Reading Comprehension

Stories of the Saints

Volume III

By Elaine Woodfield

Catholic Heritage Curricula
P.O. Box 579090, Modesto, CA 95357
www.chcweb.com 1-800-490-7713

About the Author

Elaine Woodfield has served as a Catholic school teacher, youth minister, and as a social worker advocating for the elderly and persons with disabilities. She now writes from home. She and her husband homeschool their daughter.

Dedication

This book is dedicated to
the Immaculate Heart of Mary, Queen of All Saints,
and to my husband Jim, who believed in me.

Acknowledgments

We would like to thank the Carmelite Sisters
for the photos of St. Edith Stein,

and the Society of St. Gianna Beretta Molla and St. Gianna's husband,
Pietro Molla, for the photos of St. Gianna.

ISBN: 978-0-9851642-6-3

Printed by Corley Printing
St. Louis, Missouri
July 2012
Print code: 314031

CONTENTS

Introduction   1

Apostle of Life:

Saint Gianna Beretta Molla   3

Always Go Forward, and Never Turn Back:

Blessed Junipero Serra   27

Blessed by the Truth:

Saint Teresa Benedicta of the Cross   48

With Grateful Joy:

Blessed Francis Xavier Seelos   72

Answer Key   94

How to Use the Stories of the Saints

Introduction

What is a saint? A saint is a person who lived a heroic life of love and service of God and neighbor, and who is now happy with God in Heaven. The saints are our older brothers and sisters in God's family. They are very interested in our lives, and lovingly pray for us so that we may safely reach our Heavenly home. When we ask the saints to pray for us and help us, their gratefulness knows no bounds.

The saints are for our inspiration and imitation. Each saint story illustrates how that particular saint truly lived out, or embodied, the teachings of the gospel and of the catechism. It is true that the gospel and the catechism are books that must be learned well. But even more importantly, the gospel and the catechism must truly be lived. They are books that must be "written in our hearts." The saints teach us the way to do this like good older brothers and sisters should; likewise, they inspire us to greater love and service of God and neighbor.

Vocabulary, Terms to Know

A list of vocabulary words and terms have been prepared for each story. The reader should familiarize himself with the definitions before beginning each story. In this way, the reader will understand the story better. Looking the words up builds dictionary skills. There is no need to prepare a list of dictionary-type definitions. Instead, each reader should have a good working knowledge of the word list. For example, an acceptable definition for "segregate" is "to set apart or isolate a group of people."

There are many vocabulary words and terms having to do with Catholic life and teaching. Words are important tools for our understanding of God's plan of salvation.

Comprehension Questions

The comprehension questions should be completed after the story is read. The most thorough way to learn the story is to answer the questions using complete sentences. The sequence of the questions follows the sequence of the story. The answers need not be verbatim quotes from the story, but each answer should show an accurate understanding of the story.

Although an answer key is provided, the reader's answers need not be exact. As long as the answer conveys the proper meaning, it is correct. If a reader understands the question in a different way than intended by the author, and can prove his or her answer from the text, the answer is also considered correct.

Analyze This, Essay Questions

These lesson activities encourage the reader to go beneath the surface of the stories and try to understand the heart, faith and motivation of the saints. This helps the reader to connect the saints choices with his or her own choices in life.

Quotes

Memorizing quotations of the saints is a great way to train one's memory, and it's also a great way to keep in mind a prayer or a thought for holy living! The quotation becomes part of us, as if it were "written in our heart."

Geography and History, Research and Report

Researching the geography, history of the time and country of each saint gives the reader a closer look at the saint's life. What world-rocking events did the saint have to cope with? What cultural and historical influences was the saint affected by?

You, The Biographer

Each person in the list has influenced in some way the life of the saints in these stories. Many, though divided by several centuries and different cultures, made a profound impact on the saints' lives.

Putting Your Faith into Practice

The projects are provided as ways the reader can imitate the saints in living our Faith. Not all the projects are required, though they may be completed over a four-week period if desired. These projects can be a springboard for further serious study and appreciation of the Faith.

Special Usage

A family, classroom teacher, or a homeschooling parent of a reluctant reader may wish to modify these instructions to his or her particular situation. A family may wish to do the vocabulary and comprehension questions together orally, and then choose one additional section to do together. Or else, each family member may choose his/her own preferred section to complete. Or, a family may simply want to read the stories aloud in the evening.

A classroom teacher may obtain copies for each student, and have the story read orally by students in class. Then each student may do the vocabulary and comprehension questions on paper, and choose an additional section to complete. Another approach is for the teacher to read the story to his/her class, have the class do the vocabulary and comprehension questions orally, and then do one of the additional sections as a class.

A parent of a reluctant reader may have their reader learn the vocabulary orally and answer the comprehension questions orally as well. A homeschooling family with two or more readers may want to look up the definitions and question answers as a group project, assigning a portion to each child to do but requiring that all learn the definitions and answers.

In Conclusion

My hope is that you will become interested enough in these saints to read their full biographies. If each reader makes friends with at least one saint in these stories, I will consider them a wonderful success!

Elaine Woodfield

St. Gianna Beretta Molla

Apostle of Life

Italy 1961

"I renew, to God, the sacrifice of my life. I am ready for everything, provided my child is saved."

The surgery was a success. The surgeon removed the large cyst and carefully sutured the incisions. Gianna recovered in bed, thinking of her three small children who were being cared for by friends at Courmayeur, the Molla family's favorite vacation place. She longed to join them, but wrote them letters instead: "Papa will bring you many, many kisses; I should like to come, too, but must stay in bed because I am a little ill." Gianna regained her strength, and soon, the Molla family was together again.

Gianna Beretta Molla looked ordinary at first glance. With dark, wavy hair and dark eyes, she was of average height and dressed in simple elegance in the style of the times. She looked ordinary until one noticed her smile: it was a remarkable smile, containing all the joy of living and all the kindness of a generous soul. It rarely left her face. Anyone seeing her would not suspect that within her a heroic drama was playing out between the force of life and the force of death. Always serene herself, Gianna was at the center of a controversy. She was expecting a child.

She was the mother of three children, and dearly wanted another, so the fact that a new child was on the way was very welcome news to her. Gianna Beretta Molla was herself a medical doctor, and her experience of caring for women and children told her that something was not right with her own pregnancy. After being examined by a doctor, she had an answer, and with it came a decision to make. For Gianna, it was an easy decision. In fact, she made it without hesitating for an instant. It was a heroic decision, and for this reason it deserves some explanation.

Gianna was pregnant for only one month, but along with the baby was a large tumor, or cyst, growing in her womb. It grew at a fast rate, and was increasingly painful. The doctors agreed that it would have to be removed immediately.

There were three ways to do this. First, the doctors could remove the cyst, remove the womb, and end the pregnancy, causing the death of the unborn child. Gianna would never be able to have another child. Second, doctors could remove the cyst and end the life of the unborn child; having more children in the future might be possible with this procedure. Third, the doctors could remove the cyst and let the unborn child continue to grow; Gianna chose this third option.

Unwilling to make a choice that would end the life of her child, she said to a friend, "I shall accept whatever they will do to me provided that they save the child." Gianna regarded all life as sacred, and each child as a blessing. Her vocation as a mother was a precious gift given to her by God. She wanted to have children so that they could be filled with God's grace and give glory to Him by their holy lives. For her to end the life of her child was unthinkable.

As a doctor, Gianna knew the risks of surgery during pregnancy. The cyst would be removed and the incisions would be sutured. But the growing baby and growing womb that held and nourished it would strain these sutures, as would the process of labor and delivery.

The strain on the sutures would cause ruptures, with the danger of death. When Gianna agreed to surgery, she knew she was giving up her life; for her to survive past the birth of her child would require a miracle indeed. Burdening no one with this knowledge, not even her beloved husband Pietro, she was smiling and serene. Her peacefulness convinced him that the danger was small.

Gianna prepared for surgery by receiving the sacraments. Don Luigi Galazzi, the priest of her hometown of Magenta, visited her just before she left for the hospital. He heard her confession, and gave her Holy Communion, because she wanted Jesus in the Blessed Sacrament to be her strength for this ordeal. Don Luigi encouraged Gianna to trust in God's Providence.

"Yes, Don Luigi," said Gianna, "I have prayed so much these days. With faith and hope I have entrusted myself to the Lord, even against the terrible verdict of medical science which stated: 'either the life of the mother or the life of the child; I trust in God, yes, but now it is up to me to fulfill my duty as a mother."

* * *

After the surgery, to a friend she said, "I have suffered much but I am happy because my motherhood has been saved." Gianna visited her friend, Savina Valenti, who remembers Gianna beaming with joy. "I have something beautiful to tell you," Gianna said to her. "Just imagine, I have been operated upon and I have been told that the child is safe."

Gianna continued her work as a doctor at the clinic she operated in Mesero along with her brother, Ferdinando, who also was a doctor. As always, she was a special friend of the poor, treating them for free and providing them with medicine and money; Gianna had even found new jobs for patients weakened by illness. She was a true friend to each one of her patients.

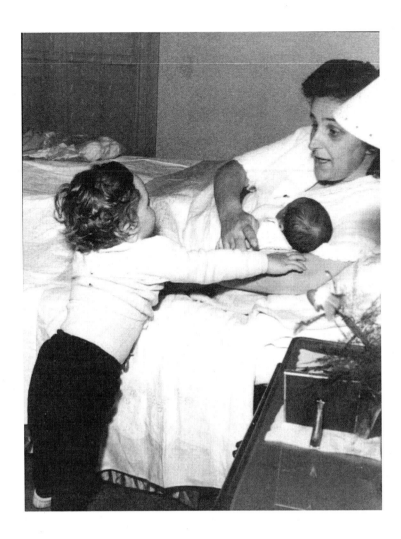

She cared for her three children (Pierluigi, age five, Mariolina, age four, and Lauretta, age two) each day except for the hours she worked as a doctor.

News spread across the countryside surrounding Mesero, carried in conversation from person to person: Dr. Gianna chose her child's life rather than her own. "Certainly God will give her a miracle because she is so generous and good," said some. Others said, "Is she crazy? She has three other children to raise! She should end the life of the child she carries so that she can take care of the others!"

What kind of mother would I be if I ended the life of my child? thought Gianna when she heard these comments. Knowing that she had made the right decision, with patience she awaited the birth of the child. Even though she had every reason to believe that she had not long to live, Gianna prayed for a miracle, as did Pietro.

Gianna had a great faith in Divine Providence – God's mysterious, loving care in all things great and small – so she remained serene in all of life's circumstances. She always said "yes" to God and "yes" to life, and this time was no exception. She did nothing by halves.

*   *   *

How did Gianna become such a noble person?

Gianna Beretta was born on October 4, 1922 in Magenta, Italy, on the feast of St. Francis of Assisi. This was a happy coincidence, since her parents Maria and Alberto were lay Franciscans, and Gianna herself put into practice the Franciscan ideals of grateful joy, simplicity, and generosity all her life. Her baptismal name was Giovanna Francesca, but she always went by Gianna.

The Beretta parents lived lives of joy and giving, and both were remembered as devout people. They always said "yes" to life, believing that all children are gifts from God. In 1908 Maria was looking over a stack of her wedding cards. One card was a cartoon drawing of thirteen beautiful, smiling children in a pot. Maria said immediately, "All!" Her wish came true.

Maria and Alberto had thirteen children, and eight of them survived infancy. Gianna was the second youngest.

A cousin of hers remembers Maria. "[As] a mother of thirteen children, she attended to each one as if she had only that one. She considered the education of her children almost a fulfillment of the work of God in His creatures, almost the creation of souls, a divine undertaking, a priesthood." Alberto was also remembered as an exemplary parent: "The great solicitude of Papa Beretta was always to keep the children attached to the family and far from occasions of sin. Honesty in his office work was scrupulous," recalled the Beretta's parish priest.

The family was well-to-do, and employed some servants to help with the work of such a large family, but they did not live as most wealthy people do. Permitting themselves few luxuries, they often gave their servants extra time off so that the Beretta children would learn to cook, clean, and look after the house themselves. The family's only real "luxury" was a good Catholic education for the children.

The Beretta parents and children went to Mass early each morning, and prayed the Rosary together each evening. One or more of the Beretta children would play the piano afterward while the others engaged in lively conversation. Maria crocheted and sewed altar linens for the missions, a cause always dear to her heart. The Beretta children got along so well with one another because they were such good friends. "The atmosphere of the home was permeated with serenity and peace," remembered Virginia, the youngest.

Once, Gianna's brother, Francisco, fell and suffered an injury that confined him to bed. Papa Beretta and his sons attended weekday Mass together and afterward accompanied the priest, along with the Blessed Sacrament he carried, to the Beretta home so that Francisco could receive Holy Communion. Mama Beretta prepared a bedside table with white cloth, crucifix, and flowers. Fr. Felice recalled: "All the boys and girls knelt with their hands joined to welcome Jesus at their home. With the Blessed Sacrament, I passed in the middle and went to the table prepared near the bed of the sick boy. The eyes of all were turned towards Jesus in the Eucharist." He always remembered the remarkable faith of the Beretta children.

Gianna was a very normal child. Virginia, her younger sister, remembered that Gianna spent a lot of time playing with her and teaching her to love what was good. Sometimes they got into mischief and were punished together.

Gianna always tried to cheer her sister up during these times, and soon the two were laughing and planning more mischief!

Gianna's oldest sister, Amalia, prepared her for her First Holy Communion. Gianna learned well from this saintly young woman who so embodied the Franciscan ideal of self-sacrifice and holy joy. After she made her First Communion at age five, she attended daily Mass with her family. Mama Beretta would wake each child in the morning with a soft caress on the cheek. Neither she nor Papa Beretta commanded the children to attend daily Mass, but left the daily choice up to each child. Nearly all of the time, the children chose to go. After Mass, Mama Beretta would stay for a while and teach the children short, beautiful prayers that she made up herself, which the children would repeat after her.

At age five, Gianna started school. There are some people who are "natural students." They remember what they learn easily, do well on tests, and always get excellent grades. Gianna was not one of them. In fact, school was a real struggle for her. She would much rather play in the outdoors among the hills and mountains of northern Italy where she lived than study in school.

But study she did. The older she got, the more she struggled. One year her grades were such that she attended summer school while the rest of the family went on their summer vacation. She wrote a letter to her sister Zita: "I have nothing else to do but study and … Amen! I am here alone, no playing!" Gianna barely passed her summer school session, but pass she did.

Education was very important in the Beretta household. The Beretta parents did not encourage good grades in their children so that they could feel superior to others. Such a thought would never occur to them. Rather, they encouraged their children in school so that each would be able to follow a profession and be Christ-like in service to others. The Beretta parents carefully chose Catholic schools for their children.

Each Beretta child benefited from such an education. Amalia lived an exemplary life and died a holy death at age twenty-six. Ferdinando became a doctor. Francisco became a civil engineer. Enrico became a doctor and a Capuchin priest and served the missions in Brazil. Zita became a pharmacologist. Guiseppe became an engineer and later a priest. Gianna became a doctor. Virginia became a doctor and a Canossian sister and served in the missions in India. The Beretta brothers and sisters were dear friends, and stayed close by letters and visits all their lives.

But all of that was to be in the years to come.

By her conduct, Gianna made a lasting impression on many people. She was a hard person to get to know, since she kept her thoughts to herself, but many people took note of her good example. Carones Cicci, a longtime school friend of Gianna, said, "Gianna had a faith so catching that all those who met her, after a short time, felt attracted to the Church, in whose life we desired to participate with deeper religiosity. Holy Mass was the basis, but we went willingly also for vespers in the afternoon and for the Rosary in the evening."

The Eucharist seems to be the key to Gianna's helpful, well-balanced, serene character. Because she received Jesus each day, she could better exemplify the virtues of Jesus in her life. "I do not remember that she had let a single day pass without receiving Holy Communion. She took part in the Eucharistic celebration even when she did not feel well!" said her brother Enrico. Making a morning meditation on He Whom she had just received, Gianna loved to think about Jesus becoming man and dying on the cross to save us.

She loved to gaze on the Crucifix. Thinking about some aspect of the life of Christ all day, she was sure to make an Eucharistic visit in the afternoon. She always carried her Rosary in her pocket or purse, and recited it daily, no matter how busy she was. To reflect on the lives of Jesus and Mary was a constant practice of hers. Since she often meditated on the life of Christ, Gianna found it easier to imitate Him. Virginia noticed this: "Her behavior was always a stimulus for good. Always attentive towards all, she forgave patiently…without manifesting to others her inmost suffering. Preoccupied not to disturb anyone, she preferred to sacrifice herself in order to see others happy."

In January of 1937, a tragedy befell the Beretta family. The eldest daughter Amalia died after a long illness. She had been a lay Franciscan like her parents, and had consecrated herself to Our Lady. Her holy life was a good example to all, and Gianna reflected on the importance of living a good life and dying a good death. The Beretta family missed Amalia's presence, and they drew even closer to one another.

Later that year, the Beretta family moved to Quinto al Mare, a suburb of Genoa, so that the older Beretta brothers and sisters could attend the University of Genoa. It was a healthy place, with hills, sea pines, orange trees and, of course, the sea itself. In this new place, Gianna's life would change.

In the spring of 1938 when she was fifteen, Gianna attended a weekend retreat. The subject of this retreat was the "Four Last Things", which are: death, judgment, heaven, and hell. Gianna knew that even though these were serious things to think about, it was very good practice to do so, because a Catholic must always be ready for death. The death of her sister emphasized this truth for Gianna. This retreat changed Gianna's life: it was as if the Holy Spirit breathed upon Gianna in a special way in this retreat.

Gianna took notes on the retreat talks, and she made a list of resolutions she composed herself:

1. I resolve to do everything for Jesus: every work of mine, every trouble, I offer all to Jesus.

2. I resolve that in order to serve God I no longer want to go to the movies if I do not know in advance whether they can be seen or not, if they are modest and not scandalous or immoral.

3. I prefer to die rather than commit a mortal sin.

4. I want to fear mortal sin as if it were a serpent and I repeat again: death a thousand times rather than offend the Lord.

5. I want to pray to the Lord that He may help me not to go to hell; hence, to avoid all that may harm my soul.

6. To say a Hail Mary daily so that the Lord may give me a happy death.

7. I pray to the Lord that He may make me understand how great is His mercy.

8. To obey M.M. [a teacher] and study even though I have no wish, for the love of Jesus.

9. From now on, every day, I shall recite my prayers on my knees, in the morning in church and in the evening in my room at the foot of my bed.

10. I want to bear up with anything … from M.M. The way of humiliations is the shortest way that leads to sanctity.

11. To pray to the Lord to let me go to heaven. To say always that I am afraid I will not go there, so I will pray and with the help of God I shall enter the Kingdom of Heaven with all the Saints and all saintly persons.

Written with her customary charming grammatical errors that would persist in her writing even when she was a doctor, Gianna's list of resolutions is a remarkable one, a true masterwork. It touches on the essentials of the Christian life. She also wrote many prayers on this retreat, resolving to say some during the day and others in the evening:

> "O Jesus, I promise to submit to everything that you may allow to happen to me; only let me know your will."

> "[I ask] the grace to understand and to do your Holy Will always; the grace to confide in you, the grace to rest securely for time and eternity in your loving divine arms."

> "O Mary, I place myself in your motherly hands and I abandon myself entirely, sure of obtaining what I ask because you are my sweet mother; I confide in you because you are the mother of Jesus. I entrust myself to you. In this trust I rest secure. … Look upon me and defend me, O sweet Mother, and at every moment of my life present me to your Son, Jesus."

These resolutions, prayers, and practices Gianna kept faithfully, and they, over time, fashioned and formed her character.

After her retreat, Gianna applied herself zealously to her studies – so zealously, in fact, that she became ill. She had to take a year off from school to regain her strength. Growing closer to her parents and benefiting by their good example made the year a sweet one for Gianna. After returning to school, she worked diligently at her studies. Whereas she had been an average student before, now Gianna excelled.

She also sought to put her retreat resolutions into practice. Gianna was not content to merely "have faith"; for her, to live a Christlike life was to serve others. There was no shortage of opportunities. It was the custom in the Beretta family at holiday time for Papa to give each child a large sum of money to spend, as each one wanted. One Christmas, Gianna and Virginia received such a gift. That very afternoon they paid a visit to a missionary institute and donated the whole amount to the missions!

Italy entered World War II in 1940, and in 1941 the Beretta family moved to Bergamo. Genoa was on the Mediterranean coast, and therefore under more wartime danger from sea and air bombardment; Bergamo was a much safer place, and it was for this reason that the family returned there. The year 1942 brought with it a double tragedy. In April Maria died of a heart ailment, and only four months later Alberto died of pernicious anemia. Losing both parents was indeed a tragedy for the Beretta brothers and sisters, but they were grateful for the good example their parents had always given them.

They kept their parents always in mind all their lives, and mentioned their example often in letters to one another.

The Beretta brothers and sisters returned to the family home in Magenta, and used this home as their "base of operations." Gianna finished secondary school. The war, with its bombardments, rationing, and general confusion, made its impact felt even in Gianna's school life. The final "School Leaving Examination" was cancelled, and Gianna was graduated on the basis of the schoolwork she had done that year. Gianna was accepted into medical school at the University of Milan.

As a medical student, Gianna spent much of her time working at her studies. How did she spend her spare time during her college student years?

First, Gianna was active in a movement called Catholic Action. The Catholic Action movement inspired its members to live a deeper spiritual life, and to put faith into action by sponsoring works of charity that served God and neighbor. Its aim was to glorify God in all things.

Gianna led activities for young people near her own age, such as retreats, country outings, plays, treasure hunts, hours of study, and spiritual conferences. Since her goal was to serve the "whole person", she organized activities of all kinds. This was very difficult during the war, since necessary goods were rationed, and travel often was interrupted due to bombardments, but somehow Gianna managed it. She had a genius for making people feel accepted, especially poorer young people who were afraid that their poverty would be looked down upon. Gianna encouraged all to love and receive Jesus in the Blessed Sacrament. She was fond of taking her friends to a country home of the Beretta family so that they could refresh body and soul.

Giving conferences to her young people was a favorite practice of Gianna. She taught them that the duty of a Catholic is to make truth visible in him or herself, and to always "be living witnesses of the greatness and beauty of Christianity." The best way to do this was by a life of purity. "How are we to preserve our purity? We must surround our bodies with the hedge of sacrifice. Purity is a virtue which is the result of much effort. ... Purity becomes beauty, and then strength and freedom. The one who is able to struggle and to stand firm is free." Gianna was a living example of the truth of her words.

"Let us always work with generosity, with humility." Gianna's vision of Catholic Action for young women was a strong one: "We should enter all fields, social, political, and that of the family. And we should work because all the forces of evil, dark and threatening have joined forces together. It is necessary that the forces of good should be united and form a dam, a barrier, so to say 'no thoroughfare.' Today, everybody who is enrolled in the Catholic Action is a soldier in the field where God has placed him. Therefore we should not be afraid because God is with us ... let us defend the Church and her ministers even at the cost of our lives..."

Realizing that a faith worth living for is a faith worth dying for, Gianna taught that faith at every opportunity. Gianna also organized activities for younger children. One photo shows her leading a large group of children on vacation. She taught them the faith by word and example.

Second, Gianna also served the poor, and she taught her young disciples to do the same. Together they visited poor people on Saturday afternoons, and helped them with their housework. They tended the sick and brought them medicines and supplies. One friend remembered that Gianna baked a birthday cake herself for a poor elderly woman she visited regularly.

She taught each of her disciples to give of himself or herself personally in direct contact with a poor person "because more than material help he feels the need of spiritual help. He feels the need of being esteemed and loved." She surrounded the poor with happiness and thoughtfulness; she would bring Virginia with her to play the accordion while she cleaned house for them!

Gianna once met up with a friend on her way home from visiting a poor woman. "Please don't keep me long; I've just bathed an old woman and I'm covered with fleas!" said Gianna with a smile and a laugh, hurrying home to shower!

Third, Gianna actively enjoyed beautiful things. She loved concerts of classical music and played the piano with skill and energy. She loved painting pictures, and was skilled in the use of color. Gianna always dressed well; she chose clothes that were simple, modest, and elegant. Gianna loved skiing in the Italian Alps not far from her home, and was an expert skier. She often said that she felt close to God when standing on top of a snowy mountain. Gianna also loved climbing mountains, ice ax in hand. She rejoiced in all the beauties of nature that she saw while skiing and mountain climbing. In Gianna was a true joy of living.

The war years were eventful ones for her. Gianna's schooling was interrupted several times due to air raids and bombardments of the war. The war ended in 1945, and that year she transferred to the University of Pavia and continued her medical studies. As always, she had to work for her academic success. She wrote to a friend, "I am going on well in my studies. It is certainly an endless examination. I have not yet finished the first volume and there are five! ... I wonder what will happen when I reach volume five. Naturally, I shall have forgotten the other four. Patience!" Her patience paid off. In January of 1950 she received her certificate to practice medicine. She continued taking classes and soon qualified to specialize in pediatrics.

Choosing to practice medicine was a "natural choice" for Gianna. Her work in Catholic Action gave her a great love of neighbor, especially her poor neighbor. Her old friend, Carones Cicci, wrote, "We were in the first year of High School and we were not thinking yet of the choice of the Faculty at the University. I was sure that Gianna would have chosen something that would bring her in contact with people for even then her thoughts were always turned to the poor, to the disowned and the sick."

Gianna was a "natural" as a doctor. In the morning, she visited her patients in their homes and in the hospital, while in the afternoons from 4:00 P. M. to 7:00 P. M. she treated patients in her office. In no time at all she became a popular and esteemed doctor. A local teacher remembers that Gianna loved her profession as a doctor, "because through it she exercised the charity of Christ; she healed and she relieved her brethren. The poor and the lowly were her favorites to whom she gave without asking anything. This testimony I have gathered from the mouths of mothers who even today speak to me about her with devoted reverence."

Regarding her profession as a mission, she made notes on one of her brother's prescription pads of her thoughts about being a doctor: "Man is a great mystery! He is body but he is also a supernatural soul. There is Jesus! He who visits the sick helps 'Me.' The priestly mission! The priest can touch Jesus, so we touch Jesus in the bodies of our patients: the poor, the young, the old, the children." Treating women and children kept Gianna close to life and its sacred origins, and so she had a great reverence for life.

But not all was smooth sailing. A man approached Gianna at her clinic to ask for medicine for his wife to abort her baby. In a rare display of anger, Gianna refused and said, "You are coming to me to ask for it?"

Another time, Gianna and her brother made a house call to a girl of seventeen who complained of abdominal pain. They questioned her, but she denied doing anything wrong. It soon became apparent that the girl had been pregnant and had acted to abort her baby. Gianna was horrified. Her dark eyes wide, she beseeched the indifferent girl in her gentle, kindly way: "Are you not sorry to have offended God thus? ... Are you really sorry for what you have done? Did you go to confession?" She was as concerned for the health of the girl's soul as she was for the health of her body.

Although Gianna was painfully aware that there are some people who will not welcome life, she was always life's apostle. In her notes, she reflects that it is never a doctor's job to end the life of an unborn child. In a crisis, the unborn child's life should be saved first, then the mother's, Gianna believed.

A local midwife, Rosa Garavaglia, who knew families all over the area, said that Gianna "improved the health of all the children through her norms of hygiene and the treatment which she gave to the mothers." Gianna was happy that she could make a difference in Magenta. Even so, she was looking to make a difference elsewhere: in the mission field of Brazil.

Gianna was truly her mother's daughter: the missions were always dear to her heart, too. What could be better that to bring the Catholic Faith to those who do not yet have it? Her brother, Enrico, was ordained a priest in 1948, taking the name Father Alberto. That same year he had left for Brazil to serve the people of its interior. Their needs were great. Francisco put his engineering degree to good use, and joined his brother in Brazil. They worked on constructing a hospital in Grajau. Gianna hoped to join them soon. What opportunities for serving others awaited her in Brazil! She sent her brothers money, supplies, medicines, and good sisterly advice by letter.

Continuing her work at her clinic, along with some work for Catholic Action, she intended to wait to be invited to come to Brazil by its bishop; then she would join her brother and work as a lay doctor consecrated to God. Time passed. Work on the hospital took longer than expected, and Fr. Alberto had time to experience first-hand all the harsh variations of the weather in Brazil. He knew Gianna had always had delicate health. He did not think that her health was up to the rigors of the Brazilian climate. Perhaps her vocation was family life, he wrote her; as a mother she could have a son who would be a priest, and in having children Gianna would be giving souls to God. Gianna knew herself well – she had her doubts, too. But with all her heart she wanted to work in the missions. What to do?

The struggle to decide her vocation took several years for Gianna. It was a painful time for her. But she knew that she had three tools to help her. The first was prayer to God for help and guidance. The second was advice from wise persons, especially her spiritual director. The third was Gianna's own mind, with its own judgment and wisdom from God.

During this time, Gianna met again and again a man with whom she was acquainted by her work in Catholic Action and as a doctor. His name was Pietro Molla, and he was an engineer who directed the SAFFA factory works. He was ten years older that Gianna, and a man of excellent character who taught catechism to the young men of his parish as his apostolate in Catholic Action. Pietro first saw her at her clinic while waiting for a doctor's appointment with her brother.

The second time he saw her, Gianna treated his sister, Teresina, in the hospital just before her untimely death. Soon he was seeing her at various Catholic Action activities, and the more he saw her, the more he fell in love with her.

Above all, Gianna wanted to do what God wanted of her. She sought His will in prayer. 1954 was a Marian Year, and in June of that year Gianna joined a pilgrimage to Lourdes. She went on the pilgrimage as a doctor accompanying the sick who wanted to ask Our Lady for the favor of a cure. Gianna had a favor of her own to ask Our Lady: what is my vocation? Her answer came in an unusual way.

She told a friend what happened just after she returned home from the pilgrimage. "I have been to Lourdes to ask Our Lady what I shall do: to go to the missions or to marry?" The

pilgrimage came to an end without an answer for Gianna, and she took the long journey home. She said. "I reached home … and Pietro came in!" Gianna regarded this as a sign from Our Lady!

Gianna and Pietro continued to see one another in Catholic Action, at the cultural center in Magenta, and at the first Mass of a newly ordained priest at Mesero. Writing of his memories of Gianna in a document addressed to her, Pietro remembered: "I remember you, when with your charming, broad smile you were congratulating Fr. Lino and his relatives. I remember you, while you were devoutly making the sign of the cross before the meal; I remember you still in prayer at the Eucharistic Blessing. I still feel the cordial clasp of your hand, and sweet and bright smile that accompanied it."

Pietro himself asked Our Lady's prayers to guide him in his own vocation. On the day after the feast of her Immaculate Conception, Pietro sensed a peace of heart that was a gift of guidance from Our Lady. After attending a ballet at the famous theater of La Scala in Milan, Gianna and Pietro rang in the new year of 1955 at the Beretta home amid relatives and friends. Pietro entrusted himself to Our Lady of Good Counsel on this day. He and Gianna continued to see one another, sharing their hopes and dreams with one another.

In February Pietro asked Gianna to marry him, and she accepted! Their great joy was to talk about the children they would have in their new family. Gianna had become convinced that just as the world has need of good missionaries, so too does it need good Christian families.

In one of the many love letters she exchanged with Pietro, she wrote of their shared desire to "do all we can to make our new family a little Cenacle where Jesus reigns over all our affections, desires, and actions."

To do this, she continued to make her morning offering: "I love you so much, dearest

Pietro, and every morning at Mass I offer my work and yours, my joys and sufferings and yours. Then I repeat the offering all day until evening."

The couple grew closer as they planned their life together. Gianna chose a wedding dress of expensive fabric. This was a strange action from a frugal woman who used only scraps of used paper and envelopes to make notes.

But Gianna explained to a friend that the fabric of her wedding dress would later be available to make a chasuble for any son of hers who would decide to become a priest! To honor God she wanted the fabric to be as fine as possible.

Fr. Guiseppe, Gianna's brother, married Gianna and Pietro on September 27, 1955. Gianna was so loved and esteemed that as she walked down the aisle the entire congregation spontaneously broke into applause that lasted until she reached Pietro at the altar. She was genuinely surprised, and "turned her big, wide-open black eyes this way and that, surprised at the clapping," remembered Pietro.

Gianna was thirty-three and Pietro forty-three when they started their life together. After a long, happy European honeymoon, they moved into a small house in Ponte Nuovo, near Pietro's work. They hoped to have four or five children at least, since they married later in life and would be older parents. They both valued children very much, considering them God's greatest blessing upon a marriage.

In 1956 their first child was born, a boy whom they named Pierluigi. Pregnancy and childbirth were difficult for Gianna; each time, her life was in danger. But each time she was also full of joy.

Remembering Pierluigi's birth, Pietro wrote, "This joy was renewed at the birth of Mariolina and again at the birth of Lauretta.

During every pregnancy, what a lot of prayers, what trust in Providence, how much fortitude in suffering! At every birth, what a hymn of thanksgiving to the Lord!"

In fact, Gianna was so thankful at the birth of each child that each time she made a sizable donation of her earnings to the missions. It was a gesture of gratitude to God. At each child's baptism, Gianna and Pietro consecrated their baby to Our Lady of Good Counsel, who was especially venerated under this title in Magenta.

Mariolina was born in 1957, and Lauretta in 1959. Running a household with several small children was a lot of work, but it was a true joy for Gianna. Pietro never saw her idle except when ill, so busy was she. Grateful for any help, she relied on a trusted servant whom she called a "domestic partner" and Pietro's mother, who was recently widowed, to help with the care of the children and the house while she worked as a doctor. Nonetheless, her children were the most important things in her life, and she structured her work life around them.

"Gianna enjoyed her children, lived for them, and was proud of them. She was so happy," Pietro said. A friend remembers a visit: "In 1961, Gianna came to me with her children. The children were talking, singing, and enjoying themselves She watched them in silence, and every now and then, she arranged the dress of one, caressed the hair of the other, and looked attentively at them. One could see that she was satisfied and proud of them."

The Molla home was known far and wide as a happy and blessed one. Gianna and Pietro were in such harmony with one another that each supported the other in any difficulty. Together they attended Mass with the children, taught them their prayers, and showed them the beauties of nature.

Their yearly vacation in the mountains of Courmayeur was always a happy one, giving Gianna a much-needed rest each summer. At home, the children loved playing in the vineyard.

Only two sorrows wrinkled Gianna's happiness. Gianna could no longer attend daily Mass since she had to get her three children up and ready for the day and for nursery school. Her sister, Virginia, said that this was a painful sacrifice for her, but that she was peaceful because she knew that caring for her children was God's will for her.

Her second sorrow was that Pietro had to travel for his job quite often. Since he flew to North America and other countries in Europe, he was gone for long periods of time. His absence was a painful sacrifice for Gianna. Air travel was much less common in those days, and Gianna feared for Pietro's safety with every flight.

Her solution was to write him many letters filled with affection and news of the children: "Kisses from my 'little man' Gigi [Pierluigi]. When by mistake a bad word slips out of his mouth, he strikes his mouth with his hand and says: 'What are you saying, Gigi?' Kisses also from my Mariolina who is becoming a 'little woman.' She helps to lay the table and does not make a mistake. Kisses from the golden-haired Lauretta who is always smiling and happy." These letters were consoling to Pietro as he anticipated joining his family once more.

And then Gianna discovered, to her great happiness, that she was expecting a child.

After the operation, Gianna's pregnancy progressed as usual. She made some plans for the future. She planned to give up her medical practice once the baby was born. Her patients always needed her, but her children needed her more, and it was time for her to devote all her energies to them.

She went through every drawer, shelf, closet, and cupboard to clean them and to put everything in good order. Ordering some fashion magazines from Paris, Gianna planned to update her wardrobe.

But she really knew that her chances were not good. She stayed smiling and serene.

"You did not say a word to me during those long months that you, as a doctor, were aware of what awaited you. And this, certainly, in order not to make me suffer," Pietro wrote later. She had chosen that her child should live, and she was faithful to life to the end.

It was time. On Good Friday, April 20, 1962, Gianna appeared at the obstetric clinic. On the way there, she reminded Pietro, "Remember, if they should ask you which of the two lives they should save, do not hesitate … first, the life of the child." She wanted them both to choose life together. As always, Pietro agreed. To the infirmarian, Sr. Maria Eugenia Crippa, she said simply, "Sister, I have come here. I have to die this time." Sister remembered Gianna gesturing with her arms downward; she looked at that moment like Our Lady on the Miraculous Medal.

At 11:00 A.M. the next morning, Gianna gave birth by caesarian section to a baby girl. With loving tenderness, she took little Emmanuela in her arms and gazed at her with love and sorrow. Already, septic peritonitis was taking its toll on Gianna. While joyful that her baby girl was born healthy, she suffered excruciating pains. These lasted for days, Gianna whispering "Mamma" when the pain became unbearable.

No less extreme was the pain of leaving her children. On Tuesday, her sister, Mother Virginia, flew in from India, and hurried to her bedside. Gianna did not even wait for her sister to cross the threshold of her sickroom before speaking to her: "At last, you are here! Ginia, if you only knew how much one suffers to have to die, leaving small children behind."

Gianna made arrangements with her sisters, Zita and Mother Virginia, to help Pietro raise her children, asking Mother Virginia to request an assignment from her order close to home for this reason.

The doctors tried everything to save her. The treatments themselves were painful. Gianna could only say, "I must live as if I were dead!"

On Tuesday night she nearly died, but her brother, Ferdinando, and sister Virginia, both doctors, saved her. Gianna had an experience she wanted to tell her husband about. On Wednesday, she told him: "Pietro, now I am healed. Pietro, I was already on the other side and if you only knew what I saw. One day, I shall tell you. But as we were too happy, too well, with our marvelous children, full of health and grace, with all the heavenly blessings, they sent me back here to suffer again, because it is not just that we should appear before the Lord without much suffering." Pietro wrote, "This has been and remains for me your bequest of joy and of suffering."

Mother Virginia gave her a crucifix; Gianna kissed it several times, just as she had taught her children to do. "If you only knew how I felt comforted in kissing the crucifix! Oh, if there were no Jesus to console us in certain moments!" Gianna said to Mother Virginia. She added, "If you knew how differently things are judged at the hour of death! … How vain certain things to which we gave importance in the world appear!"

Her sufferings increasing, Gianna repeated, "Jesus, I love you!" Unable to receive Holy Communion, she had the Host placed on her lips. She asked to go home. Finally, it was agreed. She was discharged from the hospital, and arrived home by ambulance at 4:00 A. M. on Saturday, April 28, 1962. Hearing the sounds of her children awakening, Gianna entered her last agony. She died at 8:00 A.M., only a few hours after arriving home.

At Pietro's request, the baby was baptized on Sunday with the name Gianna Emmanuela. Gianna's funeral was on the following Monday in Magenta. The town was nearly deserted that day because everyone paid their respects to Gianna. As Pietro led his children to the cemetery, Pierluigi said, "There must be a little house of gold for Mamma." Pietro was too broken with grief to respond, but he remembered. Later, he ordered a beautiful gold mosaic of Gianna presenting her baby to Our Lady of Lourdes along with Teresina for the wall of her burial chapel.

As was agreed, Gianna's sisters helped to raise her children. Mariolina died two years after her mother. Pierluigi became a businessman, married, and has children. Lauretta entered the field of economics. Emmanuela became a doctor like her mother, and treats patients with Alzheimer's Disease. She lives in Magenta with her father, Pietro.

Bl. John Paul II beatified Gianna Beretta Molla on April 24, 1994. Present at her beatification Mass were her husband, grown children, grandchildren, and her surviving brothers and sisters.

"What a heroic witness is her true chant for life, in violent contrast with a certain mentality pervasive today! May her sacrifice infuse courage in as many as participate … in the movement for life and in other similar organizations in order that the intangible dignity of every human existence be recognized, from the moment of conception up to natural decline, as a primary and fundamental value in respect to every other human and social right," said the Pope.

Three years later in Brazil, the Pope was present at the Second World Day of the Family. He listened to many speakers. One of them was Dr. Gianna Emmanuela Molla. She concluded her testimony with a prayer:

"Thank you, Mother. Thank you for having given me life twice: in conception and when you permitted me to be born, deciding for my life. Intercede so that all mothers and families may always come to you with confidence."

Listening to Emmanuela's words, the Pope wept, as did many in the large assembly.

Gianna Beretta Molla was canonized a saint by Bl. John Paul II on May 16, 2004.

May the prayers of Saint Gianna help us to always choose life!

Lesson Activities
St. Gianna Beretta Molla

Vocabulary

Define the following.

heroic	sacrament	missions	exemplify
sacred	retreat	embody	resolution
conference	Providence	profession	supernatural
console	vocation	rigor	pilgrimage
surgery	clinic	excel	life

Terms to Know

Discover the meaning of each of the following.

Catholic Action

Franciscan

Lourdes

Apostolate

Missions

Comprehension Questions

Answer the following, using complete sentences.

1. When Gianna was pregnant with her fourth child, doctors discovered a cyst in her womb. Why did they have to remove it immediately?

2. Describe the three choices that the doctors gave Gianna.

3. Why did Gianna choose the life of her child?

4. Gianna was born on the feast of St Francis of Assisi. Why is this a happy coincidence?

5. Although the Beretta family was well off, they did not live as wealthy people do. What was the family's only luxury?

6. Why did the Beretta parents encourage their children in school?

7. What was the key to Gianna's character?

8. When Gianna was fifteen, she attended a retreat that changed her life. What was the subject of this retreat?

9. What were three ways that Gianna spent her spare time when she was a college student?

10. Gianna was a "natural" as a doctor. What two choices of vocation did she struggle with?

11. What three tools helped her in this struggle?

12. Finish this sentence: Gianna had become convinced that just as the world has need of good missionaries …

13. Gianna missed Pietro when he was gone on business trips. What was her solution for this difficulty?

14. On the way to the hospital, Gianna reminded Pietro to choose the life of the child first. Why did she do this?

15. In 1997 in Brazil, what was Emmanuela's prayer?

Analyze This

Using as many details as you can, explain each question in paragraph form.

1. How did Gianna finally excel at her studies?

2. Why did Gianna choose to become a doctor?

3. As a doctor, how did Gianna cope with those who would not accept life?

4. How did Gianna take steps to resolve her vocation question?

5. How did the Molla family life embody the values of Gianna and Pietro?

6. In her last pregnancy, what made Gianna choose the life of her child?

Essay Questions

Answer one or more of the following in essay form.

1. How did Gianna's family influence her to become a devout and heroic person?

2. What strategies did Gianna use to come to her decision to marry Pietro?

3. How did the resolutions Gianna made from her retreat change her life?

4. How did Gianna regard the poor?

5. Why did Gianna make every effort to attend daily Mass?

6. Describe the family life of Gianna, Pietro, and their children.

7. Describe Gianna's spiritual life.

8. Why is Gianna's choice for the life of her child seen as a difficult one?

9. If Gianna had chosen to save her own life instead of that of her child, what might have been some repercussions of this choice in her own life, in her family life, and in her profession?

10. How is Gianna's list of retreat resolutions a good blueprint for the Christian life?

Quotes

Complete one or more of the following.

1. Choose one or more quotes from St. Gianna, memorize it/them, and recite it/them.

2. Choose a quote from St. Gianna and explain it in essay form. You may wish to give your composition as a speech.

3. Study the words of Bl. John Paul II at Gianna's beatification Mass, and comment on them in essay form. What does he say about human dignity? You may wish to give this composition as a speech.

Geography and History

Complete one or more of the following.

1. Using the place names in this biography, draw and label a map of the life of St. Gianna.

2. Research and draw a map illustrating Italy's experience of World War II.

3. What drew Italy into the war? Were its people behind its leader? What was the final outcome of the war for Italy? Research and write a report answering these questions.

4. Gianna spent much of her life near Milan. Research and write a report on one or more of the following:

   a. Milan and its history

   b. Famous people of Milan

   c. Milan today: its points of interest

5. Draw a map and write a brief report on the Italian Alps.

Research and Report

Choose one or more of the following topics, and research and write a report about it. Be sure to include related maps, diagrams, time lines, and illustrations.

1. Italy, Ancient and Modern.

2. Lay Franciscans (also known as Third Order Franciscans)

3. The Catholic Action Movement.

4. The Miraculous Image of Our Lady of Good Counsel

You, The Biographer

Research and write a biography of one or more persons listed below. Be sure to use at least two sources for your biography. You may wish to present it as a speech.

1. St. Francis of Assisi

2. St. Elizabeth of Hungary (patroness of lay Franciscans)

Putting Your Faith into Practice

Choose one or more of the following.

1. Write an essay or speech telling how the life or St. Gianna Beretta Molla inspires you to live a deeper Christian life.

2. Point for point, comment on Gianna's retreat resolutions. Why does she make each one? What does she wish to accomplish? What does she want to avoid? Why is each one a good idea? You may comment in written form, or present your comments as a speech.

3. Develop a service plan for helping someone you know in need, and carry out your plan.

4. Look into various pro-life organizations and activities in your area, and support one of them with your time as a volunteer or with donations. Look for ways to educate others on pro-life issues, and most of all, look for ways to educate yourself.

5. Gianna prayed for a miracle. Fernanda Garegnani from Magenta said, "The Lord has worked the miracle, but a miracle all His own – rather, He has multiplied them. With the heroic death of Dr. Gianna, He wished to make many mothers understand that the life of each one is a precious gift which is very often 'thrown away' carelessly by so many women who do not know what it means to be 'a mother.' Gianna knew it, and that is why she gave her life for her children."

Write an Essay or Speech

1. Commenting on the above quote.

2. Answering the question: What is motherhood?

3. Answering the question: How is St. Gianna a good example for mothers?

4. Answering the question: What good has come out of St. Gianna's sacrifice?

Science and Life

1. Research and write a report on the stages of development of an unborn child. Illustrate each stage by drawing or by copying actual photographs.

2. The use of contraception and abortion has had a significant effect on the population and its rate of growth. Select one of the following and research and write a report on:

   a. the declining population rate throughout the world

   b. the drop in the birth rate since 1960 (which was the year that the contraceptive pill was put on the market)

   c. the Roe vs. Wade Supreme Court decision that legalized abortion

   d. the statistics of abortion

   e. economic repercussions of a declining population

3. Read the papal encyclical *Humanae Vitae (On Human Life)* and:

   a. summarize it in report form

b. report on the prophetic nature of the encyclical. In other words, how have the problems predicted by Pope Paul VI at the end of the encyclical come true in our day?

4. Explain in your own words why abortion and contraception are evil. Do this as if you were reasoning with a person of your age level.

For more information, holy cards,
or to report favors received, please contact:

Saint Gianna Beretta Molla Society
P.O. Box 2946
Warminster, PA 18974
www.saintgianna.org

Blessed Junipero Serra

Always Go Forward, and Never Turn Back

December 1749

The Caribbean Sea off the Coast of Mexico

It was the worst ocean storm that the ship's crew had ever seen. Strong north winds and heavy seas battered the ship *Villasota* for many days, and the sailors and passengers did not know how much more the ship could take. It seemed as if crewmen were everywhere working frantically; some were operating pumps, others were repairing the damaged timbers of the ship, while still others were trying to secure the cargo that the storm had shaken loose.

The ship and crew were a valiant lot, but they were no match for the storm. The captain had let the ship drift with the storm winds in an attempt to save her, but now it was no use. The main mast looked like it was split and ready to break away and the pumps began to give out.

"Captain! Run her aground!" came a shout over the noise of the storm.

"Yes! Run her aground, sir! If she rests on the shore, it might give us time to save our skins!" another crewman joined in. Other voices agreed, shouting to be heard.

The captain listened and appeared to ponder what his crew were saying. All knew that this was a drastic step. If they ran the ship aground, it would be completely lost; crew and passengers could also be lost in the attempt to reach safety.

Only one man remained serene. In fact, he looked as if he were sailing on a ship under clear skies and gentle breezes. He was dressed in the gray robes of a Franciscan priest. His name was Fr. Junipero Serra. He was a missionary traveling with other missionaries on his way to serve the Indians of the New World. Little did anyone suspect that he would change the face of the New World.

"Aren't you afraid, Father?" asked Fr. Palou, one of his fellow missionaries.

"I was a little afraid at the beginning," admitted Fr. Serra, "but the thought of the ideal that is leading us to the Indies got the better of my fright at once." Fr. Palou understood what Fr. Serra meant.

Their whole purpose of coming to the New World was to bring the Gospel to the Indians; if it were truly God's will that they do so, He would surely protect them. If they happened to lose their lives in the attempt, then at least they could offer their lives as a sacrifice so that others who would come later would find success.

"The blood of the martyrs is the seed of the Church," thought Fr. Palou. When someone dies for the Faith, blessings are sure to follow. Still, they should fight for life until the very end. Fr. Serra had an idea. He began handing out scraps of paper to the other Franciscans.

"Write the name of your favorite saint on this paper," he said. After they did so, he collected the papers in an urn. "We'll draw out a name, and ask that saint to help us." The priests watched as he drew one piece of paper out of the urn. Fr. Serra unfolded it.

"The honor of helping us goes to St. Barbara!" he announced. The other Franciscans nodded. They knew that today happened to be her feast day. Was this God's way of telling them to have confidence?

Together they prayed the prayer to the Holy Spirit and to all the saints. Then they said as loudly as they could, "Viva Santa Barbara!" ("Long live St. Barbara!") All of a sudden, the roaring wind died down, and soon became gentle. The rough seas stopped pounding on the hapless ship. The storm had merely gone away!

The relieved crew got the ship ready in record time, and they sailed on to Veracruz. The captain was amazed to find that the winds of the storm had pushed the ship closer to their destination.

After they disembarked, the Franciscans told the story of what had happened to their fellow priests who were already serving in Mexico. They listened to the story in amazement. There was only one thing to do: they all sang a Mass of thanksgiving in honor of St. Barbara. The age of miracles was indeed not past. Was there another saint among them?

Veracruz is on the Caribbean coast of Mexico. Ahead of the Franciscan fathers was a journey overland of over two hundred miles to Mexico City, the capital. All but two of them set out on the journey by mule train. Fr. Serra and a companion decided to walk the whole way as a penance for the success of the Mission to the New World.

Reading the lives of the saints had inspired Fr. Serra to bring the Christian faith to the natives of the New World as well as to be ready to give his life for them. What could be better than to give precious souls to God? His desire for sacrifice was soon to be rewarded. During his walking journey, an insect bit his leg. During the following night, he scratched the wound in his sleep, and awoke with a raging infection. The wound would never heal, and he would be lame from it from that time on. He would bear the wound and infection for the rest of his life. Some think that the insect that bit Fr. Serra was a mosquito, while others think that it was a scorpion. The best evidence suggests that it was a brown spider whose bite was sometimes fatal; people would often lose the limb that was bit to gangrene. Fr. Serra was blessed by God with a penance.

He and his companion received help of an unusual kind on their journey to Mexico City. They came across a river that they needed to cross, but the current was swift and the river appeared to be deep. They looked for a shallow place where they could ford the river, but they could not find one. They stood looking at the river, trying to figure out what to do next, when they heard someone speak.

"Do you need to cross the river? Come with me. I know a good place," said a stranger who seemed to appear from nowhere. The man was dressed in traveling clothes, and seemed friendly and helpful. What did they have to lose? They followed the man a short distance along the riverbank. He stopped and pointed to a place in the river.

"This place is very shallow. You will have no trouble crossing the river there," he said. The two Franciscans stared at the place in the river to which he pointed; it looked as deep as the rest of the river.

Nonetheless, they prepared to cross. They found that the river was indeed very shallow in that place, and they crossed it with no difficulty at all. They turned to thank the helpful stranger on the opposite bank, only to find that he had disappeared!

Another day, Fr. Serra and his companion found that their food supply was completely gone. They had traveled long and hard that day, and found themselves far from civilization of any kind. They looked around for edible plants, but not finding any, they settled themselves for a hungry night in the open. All of a sudden, a stranger appeared.

"Are you hungry?" he asked. Just like the man at the river, this stranger was dressed as a traveler, and he seemed kind. "Yes, we are very hungry," answered the two priests. They wondered what farm or village he had come from, and what he was doing so far from home as night was about to fall. He would not tell them where he came from, but instead offered them a strange-looking fruit.

"Here. Try this. You will find that it will quench your thirst, too," said the stranger. They took the fruit from him and tasted it doubtfully. It was delicious and juicy. As they turned to thank him, he was no longer there. Looking for him among the rocks and desert plants nearby, they could not find him. They returned to their camp and finished the fruit, remarking how unusually delicious it was. They were surprised to find how full they were.

Still another day, the Franciscans found that they were out of food again in a desolate place. Another stranger rode up on horseback and spoke to them. "You must be hungry! Here, I have something that you will like," he said, offering them some food that looked at first like cornbread. Looking closer, the bread looked as if it were only half-baked. The fathers were reluctant to eat any of it, knowing that raw dough would make them sick. Seeing their hesitation, the stranger on horseback encouraged them to eat.

"Go ahead! It will not hurt you!" he said. Reluctantly, they tasted the bread. It was delicious, and tasted like the finest cream-filled pastry they had ever eaten! Turning to thank the man, they saw, like the two others before him, that he was gone.

Finally, they reached the Apostolic College of San Fernando in Mexico City, which was the headquarters of the Franciscan Missionaries in the New World. Fr. Serra brushed up on his studies for missionary work. His missionary zeal inspired everyone at San Fernando.

Making a play-on-words with Fr. Junipero Serra's first name, one of the older fathers said, "I wish God would send us a forest of Junipers!" The day was coming soon when Fr. Serra would be sent to the Indians whom he was so eager to serve.

Who was Fr. Junipero Serra?

He was born in the town of Petra on the island of Mallorca, off the Spanish coast, on November 24, 1713, and was given the name Miguel José. His devout parents, Antonio and Margarita, made sure that he received the sacrament of Baptism on the same day he was born.

The family attended the church of St. Bernadine, which was served by Franciscan priests; the Serra family was known as a happy and holy one. The family spent much time at St. Bernadine, and from his earliest years young Miguel wanted to be a Franciscan. This desire grew in the warm and fertile climate of Mallorca. Miguel always had poor health, but he was very intelligent, so his parents sacrificed to send him to school. He was not suited for the hard manual labor needed to survive as a farmer.

When Miguel was sixteen years of age, he entered the Franciscan seminary. He learned well. His favorite reading material was the lives of the saints, and his greatest desire was to imitate them. His dearest wish was to convert sinners, even at the price of shedding his own blood for them, if need be. This desire to sacrifice himself for others was to grow in him all his life, and it led him to attempt great things because he was not concerned with himself and his own survival or glory. In doing all for God, he did not count the cost.

Miguel made his profession as a Franciscan on September 15, 1731, and took the name Junipero, after Brother Juniper, who was such a close friend of St. Francis of Assisi. Miguel had always been very short of stature, so short that he looked like a child. After his profession, be began to grow more normally, and he always said that it was the grace of his Franciscan profession that made him grow.

He studied for the priesthood and was ordained a priest. He gave his parents credit for his vocation, saying it was their prayers and good example that made his priestly vocation possible. He returned to his home village to offer Mass there as often as he could; what better way was there than Holy Mass to thank these good parents for all they had done? Fr. Junipero was brilliant in scholarship, and soon became a professor of philosophy and a doctor of sacred theology.

He taught at the Franciscan seminary, and preached at the different parishes of the island. He was happy to serve God as a priest, but still, he wanted to be a missionary. He prayed for the chance to become one, and finally his chance came.

Word came from New Spain (now known as Mexico) that more missionaries were needed to preach to the Indians there. Any priest who wanted to be a missionary to the New World must make a commitment to serve in that capacity for at least ten years. Fr. Junipero requested that he be sent, but his superior was reluctant to lose such a good seminary teacher. So priests gathered at the seaport, waiting for the ship that would take them to the New World. Fr. Junipero was not among them.

Five priests from Andalusia, a mountainous region, arrived at the port. They took one look at the vastness of the ocean, which they had never seen before, and became frightened at its immensity. They decided to remain in Spain rather than risk a long sea voyage to the New World. There were five new openings now. Fr. Junipero's superior gave him the necessary permission, and he prepared to depart for Spain. He did not return to his family to say good-bye, knowing that his love for them and theirs for him might make him waver in his decision. His example inspired several friends and former students to join him. He sailed from Mallorca to Malaga to Cadiz to the New World.

*   *   *

Fr. Serra was finally going to realize his dream of bringing the faith to the Indians of the New World. At the time he arrived, Mexico City and many other large cities were predominantly Catholic, but Indians in outlying areas knew only the rudiments of the faith. The fact that the Christian faith spread in Mexico at all was truly miraculous. Before the Spanish came, Aztec Indian civilization was in a deplorable state. It is true that the Aztecs were a very advanced race, and built fine buildings, constructed a system of aqueducts and irrigation channels, and made fine handcrafts, which they traded with other tribes and peoples. The flat-topped pyramids that they built were marvels of architecture. But the Aztecs practiced human sacrifice on a truly astonishing scale.

The Aztecs did not sacrifice their own people, but did sacrifice slaves and the people of other tribes whom they conquered in battle. The false god they worshipped required daily sacrifice of human hearts, so the Aztecs made war constantly on other tribes so that they would always have a fresh batch of people to sacrifice. These they kept imprisoned in stockades everywhere in their land.

After the sacrifice atop the pyramid was complete, the Aztecs prepared the remains to be cannibalized. This insured a ready food supply. Observers of the time estimated that tens of thousands of people were sacrificed each year. A special occasion like the dedication of a new temple called for the sacrifice of twenty thousand people in a single day. The Aztecs also murdered one another, it seems, for no reason at all except that it was somehow entertaining for them.

At a loss to explain the gruesome behavior of an entire people, one Spanish observer decided that the Aztecs were not human. Others more accurately concluded that the Aztecs as a people were somehow possessed.

Our Blessed Lady herself appeared to one of these Aztec converts in 1521 to ask that a church be built on a spot that formerly had been a place of such sacrifice. She also indicated that the Indians were dear to her, and that she would pray for them. She left a miraculous picture of herself dressed in Aztec royal colors that survives to this day. The story of the apparition of Our Lady of Guadalupe served to convert eight million Indians in only a few short years. The Indians proved to be fervent Catholics, but there were not enough missionaries to go around.

Fr. Serra was sent to serve the Pame Indians of the Sierra Gorda Mountains along with several other priests of whom he was made their superior. He served there for nine years. The territory to which they were sent was a large area with many parishes. The Pame Indians had been baptized but rarely received any sacraments due to the shortage of missionaries. At once Fr. Serra set himself to learn their language, and he led public prayers and taught the Indians in their own language. Gradually he introduced them to Spanish, teaching them the Spanish version of the prayers they knew, and by and by they learned Spanish, too.

Fr. Serra himself lived a very austere life; he slept little, preferring to spend his nights in prayer, and when he did sleep, he did so on a bed made of boards and used little covering. He also ate sparingly. He believed in celebrating the sacraments with as much splendor as possible. After all, nothing was too good for God Himself! Fr. Serra managed to acquire beautiful vestments and chalices as well as paintings, crosses, and statues. Holy Mass was an occasion for as much reverence and splendor as possible. He put on dramas and pageants in which the Indians themselves took part in order to dramatize for them the events of the life of Christ.

The main feasts of the Church year required special attention; there was a large pageant at Christmas time, and on Holy Thursday Fr. Serra reenacted the Last Supper in every detail, including the washing of the feet, when he assembled the oldest and most respected Indian men for this honor. He erected a large crucifix for Good Friday, and had the Body of Christ taken down from the cross in a dramatic and realistic way using a series of ropes and pulleys. Fr. Serra regularly led a Rosary procession in which everyone took part, and he taught his parishioners a great confidence in the prayers of the Mother of God. Other Indians joined the Church, attracted by the splendor of worship that fed their souls.

The Pame Indians lived a subsistence life as nomads, so Fr. Serra taught them to plant and harvest crops; the Indians became so proficient at this that soon they were trading the surplus crops they grew for other necessities.

He and the missionaries taught the men the arts of bricklaying and building construction, carpentry, and blacksmithing; the women learned to weave and sew clothing. Fr. Serra, along with the Indians, built a church at Jalpan that is still in use to this day. The Pame Indians were such committed Catholics that they voluntarily gave Fr. Serra a white stone idol they used to worship so that they would not be tempted to return to pagan practices.

In 1758 Fr. Serra's superiors recalled him to Mexico City, and assigned him to give parish missions; he did this for almost nine years. He lived at San Fernando for some of each year, teaching at the seminary and giving spiritual direction; the other part of each year he was on the road, walking from place to place, giving parish missions. He was a good preacher who could move his listeners to true repentance for their sins, and he was much in demand as a confessor. Fr. Palou, who accompanied him for most of his missionary life and was later his biographer, estimated that during these years he walked over five thousand miles. His bad leg was often swollen and sore, but he did not let this deter him.

Fr. Serra's years as a parish missioner were not without their dangers. Once, someone poisoned the wine Fr. Serra used at Mass; he did not die as expected, but merely lost his power of speech and recovered fairly quickly.

"And if they shall drink any deadly thing, it shall not hurt them." Fr. Serra quoted these words from the Gospel of Mark as soon as he regained his speech. He heard confessions and preached that evening as if nothing had happened!

One evening, he and a companion traveled back to San Fernando after giving a parish Mission. The sun had set before they could reach the place where they had planned to spend the night. In fact, they were in the middle of nowhere. Taking one last look around before preparing to sleep in the open, they saw a small house with three cottonwood trees standing together in front of it. A dignified man, his young wife and small son welcomed them gladly. They could see that the house, although poor, was very neat and clean inside. The family insisted that the Franciscan priests accept a meal from them; after they had eaten, the family prepared a comfortable place for them to sleep. The fathers were struck by the peaceful kindness of the family, and loved to watch the young boy playing quietly on the clean swept floor. They felt a wonderful peace while they were guests of the family. In the morning, they bade them farewell, and went on their way.

Soon they met up with some men on horseback who were also traveling. "Where did you fathers spend the night? There is no house for many miles here," asked one of them, puzzled.

"Over there by those three cottonwoods," said Fr. Serra, "there is a house where a family gave us a kind welcome."

The men on horseback looked at one another. "There is no house there, father. There are no people living here for many miles around. I know this area well," said one of them. It was the fathers' turn to be puzzled. To solve the mystery, they all went back to the house. But the house was not there. In fact, there was no trace of any home at all. The only things that remained were the three cottonwood trees that stood together! Fr. Serra and his companion concluded that it was the Holy Family who had given them hospitality, and they gave thanks to God for His loving Providence.

In 1768, Fr. Serra traveled to Baja (Lower) California to serve as president of the missions there. The previous year, the king of Spain issued a decree that expelled the Jesuit missionaries from Spain and all her colonies; he gave no reason why. The Jesuits wished that their missionary work continue, so the Franciscans traveled to take over the missions begun by the Jesuits. In the mean time, the missions were left in the hands of the Spanish army; the idea was that the army guard the missions from theft and vandalism by the Indians. In fact, the soldiers stole from and harmed the missions far more than the Indians ever could. When Fr. Serra and his fellow Franciscans arrived, they found the missions in a deplorable state.

To add insult to injury, the army officials would not permit the Franciscan fathers to use any supplies at the missions. The whole situation was a recipe for failure. In addition, the terrain of Baja California was rocky, hot, and dry. Despite all this, Fr. Serra and his fellow priests did their best to preach the Gospel and bestow the sacraments.

That same year, the Inspector General of New Spain, sent by the Spanish king himself to oversee the progress of his colony in the New World, arrived in Mexico. His name was Don José de Galvez. He was appalled at the difficult conditions in which the missionaries worked, and commanded immediately that all belongings of the missions be turned over to the missionaries. He proved to be a good ally for Fr. Serra. He received orders from Spain that were to change the life of Fr. Serra forever.

He must arrange an expedition to occupy Upper Baja California for Spain.

There were two reasons for this. First, the Spanish looked upon Upper California (our present state of California) as its own territory. They explored its coast by sea as early as 1542. In 1595, the explorer, Ceremeno, anchored his ship in a bay north of San Francisco, came ashore, and planted the Spanish flag to claim the land for Spain. In 1602 Vizcaino also explored the coast, going ashore twice and naming the places Monterey (The King's Mountain) and San Diego. The Spanish crown decided that it was high time to explore and settle this land that was part of its domain. Second, the Russians had discovered Alaska in 1741, and had built fishing and trapping settlements along its coast. They started to build their settlements further south, and the Spanish crown was worried that the Russians might try to encroach upon the territory they considered their own. To prevent this, they were going to occupy Upper California themselves.

Galvez planned to make two land and two sea expeditions, intending all four expeditions to rendezvous at the site of San Diego. Galvez was so dedicated to these plans that he himself helped to caulk the ships and pack cargo for travel. Upon learning of these plans, Fr. Serra offered a Mass of Thanksgiving, and urged his fellow missionaries by letter to do the same. Fr. Serra would travel with one of the groups traveling by land. The ship *San Carlos* set out in January of 1769 and the ship *San Antonio* sailed in February. Fr. Serra spent time visiting his Baja missions and gathering the supplies he would need to establish missions in Upper California. Fr. Serra visited Fr. Palou, who was to take his place as president of the Baja missions. Fr. Palou was shocked at the state of Fr. Serra's leg: it was covered with sores and was swollen.

"Fr. Serra, you should let me go in your place!" said the compassionate Fr. Palou.

"Let us not speak of that," answered Fr. Serra. "I have placed all my confidence in God, through whose goodness I hope to be permitted to reach not only San Diego, in order to plant and establish the standard of the Holy Cross at that port, but Monterey as well."

They started out in early May, and the trip by land was not an easy one. The expedition traveled by mule train. Fr. Serra, so used to walking, was unable to do so. His leg was in such bad shape that two men had to help him on and off a mule. Then he could not even sit upright, and had to be carried by stretcher, and could not celebrate Mass. He called an experienced muleteer to his side.

"I have a favor to ask of you," said Fr. Serra.

"What would you like me to do?" asked the muleteer. He, like the rest of the people in the expedition, liked and esteemed Fr. Serra, and was worried about him.

"I would like you to prepare the same poultice that you give your mules when they go lame, and apply it to my bad leg," said Fr. Serra.

"But Father, you are no mule!" said the muleteer with a smile.

"Would you do it anyway?" asked Fr. Serra.

The muleteer agreed, and gathered the medicinal herbs he used to treat his mules. He mixed them with some warm tallow, and applied the poultice to Fr. Serra's leg. Falling asleep immediately, Fr. Serra awoke feeling well the next morning and celebrated Mass as though nothing was wrong. The people of the expedition watched him with amazement. Was this God's way of rewarding the humility of a man who would not hesitate to use a mule's remedy?

The land expedition arrived at San Diego on July 1, 1769. The other three expeditions had preceded them. Each expedition had many stories to tell of the hardships along the way. Both of the ships lost many sailors to disease; when one of them arrived in San Diego, only four sailors could stand upright.

On July 16, Fr. Serra blessed and erected a large Mission cross, and offered Holy Mass in a temporary chapel to dedicate the Mission of San Diego. It was the first of nine missions he was to found in the next fifteen years of his life. Some Indians watched the ceremony with curiosity. Fr. Serra prayed that he and his missionaries would bring many of these souls to God.

The Indians seemed to know that they had a friend in Fr. Serra, and before long, they would crowd around him. They were not interested in food, for the region was a fertile one and they were well fed. They were fascinated with cloth. The Indians had never seen the like before. The men wore no clothing and the women clothed themselves modestly with woven rushes. The Indians considered cloth a treasure and would do anything to possess or even touch it. So they found Fr. Serra's gray Franciscan habit interesting, and would ask him for it often. They liked to pass his spectacles among themselves, which made Fr. Serra anxious, but they always returned them.

Some of the women would give him their babies to hold, and would laugh with joy as he took them. The Indians lived as hunters and gatherers, and had no idea of agriculture or raising livestock at all.

Converting them to the faith proved to be difficult. In the first year, there were no converts at all. Disease was claiming more and more Spaniards, and the Indians watched as the Spaniards became fewer in number. In August they attacked the Mission, killing one man and injuring another. They stole whatever they could, and disappeared into the hills. Fr. Serra urged the soldiers not to retaliate. Later the Indians offered one of their infants for baptism. Just as Fr. Serra was about to pour holy water upon the child's head, the Indians snatched it away and departed without explanation. Why had this happened? Were the Indians frightened? Or had they intended to do this all along? None of these questions had an answer. Such setbacks would serve to discourage a lesser man, but not Fr. Serra.

"I put my trust in the Lord who created them and redeemed them with the most precious Blood of His Son; He will bring them to the fold in the manner and at the time that He will be pleased to do so," he wrote.

The ship *San Antonio* had returned to Baja California for supplies that were badly needed. The San Diego Mission and its residents were in a dreadful state. Portola, the governor of Baja California and the leader of Fr. Serra's expedition, decided that if the *San Antonio* had not returned by the Feast of St Joseph (March 19), they would all go back to Baja California for good.

Fr. Serra would not hear of going back. "I shall remain here alone with Fr. Juan Crespi and hold out to the very last," he wrote. He began a novena of prayers to St. Joseph, asking him to pray for the success of the Mission. He was willing to give his own life for its success.

On the feast of St. Joseph, they spotted the sail of the *San Antonio* on the horizon. Two days later it sailed into harbor. It had been on its way to Monterey to meet up with an exploration expedition, but lost its anchor and came to San Diego instead. Fr. Serra gave thanks that the prayers of St. Joseph saved the whole Mission to Upper California just in the nick of time!

From that time on, Fr. Serra established missions at a rapid pace. The next year, in 1770, Fr. Serra founded the Mission San Carlos Borromeo at Carmel, near Monterey, in California; this became his headquarters. He founded the Mission San Antonio south of Carmel in 1771, and traveled south, founding the Mission San Gabriel the same year.

Fr. Serra founded the Mission San Luis Obispo, midway between Los Angeles and San Francisco, in 1772, and Mission San Juan Capistrano in 1776. That same year he founded the Mission San Francisco, and in 1777 he founded the Mission Santa Clara. The last Mission he founded was San Buenaventura in 1782. Fr. Serra made plans to found the Mission Santa Barbara, and did erect and bless the large Mission cross on its site, as he did with each Mission he founded, but did not live to do so. The missions were about thirty miles apart, the distance of a day's walk, and linked together by a road called El Camino Real (The Royal Way).

There were over one hundred different groups of Indians in Upper California, each with a different language. They lived in very primitive conditions. Their villages were only small groupings of huts that the Indians would burn down when they became too full of vermin; then they would build new ones. Some tribes were warlike, attacking anyone who had goods they wanted. Some were peaceful, and others were afraid to travel far for fear of attack by other Indians. Raising crops and livestock animals were unknown to California Indians; they survived on the roots, nuts, and plants they could gather. Polygamy was common, as was divorce, although some tribes maintained loving and committed families. In some tribes, the men slept sixteen hours a day, except for hunting time, while the women did all the work and were otherwise mistreated. Idol worship was unknown to California Indians. Many tribes wove beautiful baskets, and were skilled at making good use of the food they had. The expertise of the hunters at stalking game greatly impressed the Spaniards.

Fr. Serra's heart ached for the Indians and their hard life, and he wanted to improve their lives as well as save their souls. Founding missions was the best way to do both for them. His method was simple. He found a good piece of ground near the sea, since ships would be giving them supplies from Mexico for a while until the Mission could sustain itself. He erected a large Mission cross and blessed it in a moving ceremony.

Fr. Serra was forced to temporarily abandon one Mission cross. When he returned, he found that the Indians there who had so resisted the Faith now fervently wanted to accept it. He also found many offerings of food and gifts at the foot of the cross. What had made them change?

"At night this cross was lit up from within, and glowed so we could see it from a great distance," they managed to communicate to him through an Indian interpreter. "We know that you Spanish wear crosses around your necks. This glowing cross is a great wonder. This God of yours must have great power, and so we offer gifts as homage to Him." Fr. Serra could but give thanks for this unexpected miracle and for the great faith of the Indians.

Before there were even buildings at Mission San Antonio, Fr. Serra hung the Mission bells from the branches of a tree and began to ring them loudly.

"Come, Gentiles, come to Holy Church! Come and receive the faith of Jesus Christ!" he called out. Another priest was amused at this. "There are no Indians in sight, Father," he said. Fr. Serra answered, "I can hear them coming," referring to the future. And later, they came!

Buildings quickly followed the Mission cross. At first these were made of wood, but after several disastrous fires started by flaming arrows during battles with warlike Indians, they were built of stone and tile was used for the roofs. The buildings included a church, quarters for the priests, barracks for soldiers, rooms for unmarried women, workshops, dining rooms and kitchen, and storage buildings. Each Mission was shaped in a quadrangle so that it could be more easily defended in time of attack.

Fr. Serra would make friends with the Indians who came out of curiosity to see what was going on. He tried to learn important words of their language and was courageous enough to stumble along in the Indians' language; this caused peals of good-natured laughter from the Indians as he tried to pronounce the new words he was learning. He tried to teach Spanish to the Indians, succeeding most with the children.

Fr. Serra made sure that each Mission had Catholic art so to aid in teaching the Indians the faith. At one Mission, he unveiled a picture of Our Lady holding the Child Jesus. Never having seen a picture before, the Indians thought that the image was real, and gazed at it for a long time. The Indian women thought that the Child looked too thin, and compassionately offered to nurse Him themselves!

At another Mission, the Indians were not so friendly. They were warlike, and threatened the Spaniards. Fr. Serra put a picture of the Sorrowful Mother holding her Son Jesus, taken down from the Cross, in a prominent place.

The Indians stopped their threats immediately and gathered to gaze upon the face of the Sorrowful Mother. After that, they would come and place food and handcrafts at the foot of the picture to console Mary in her sorrow. It seems that God was pleased with the Indians' compassion for the Sorrowful Mother. Large numbers of them asked to be instructed and baptized, and they became fervent and exemplary Catholics.

Fr. Serra taught the Indians that the Son of God loved them, came to earth for them, and died to free them from sin. Our Lord Jesus wanted to bless them with grace in this life and take them to heaven when they died. Philosophical argument did not interest the Indians, so Fr. Serra put on plays, pageants, and processions to teach them the Catholic Faith. He saw great value in learning by doing. The Indians loved to participate in these, especially the children.

Indians interested in baptism came each morning for instruction, and Fr. Serra had them repeat their lessons for better memorization. The decision to be baptized was left to each person; to compel someone to receive baptism is never permissible. But a surprising number voluntarily joined the Church, and it is estimated that Fr. Serra welcomed over five thousand Indians into the Church in his lifetime. They had a deep affection for him. A day in which he came to visit a Mission personally was a festive one.

Fr. Serra had a way of making sure that each person, be they Indian or Spaniard, knew that they were very important to God and to him. What impressed people the most about Fr. Serra was the devout and fervent way in which he celebrated Holy Mass. He obtained beautiful vestments, chalices, statues, and pictures for all of his Mission churches. Fr. Serra was very reverent in the presence of the Blessed Sacrament. It was easy to believe that Holy Mass was the closest thing on earth to heaven when Fr. Serra celebrated it.

The Indians longed to receive Jesus in the Blessed Sacrament, and the day of an Indian's First Communion was a day so special that he or she remembered it for the rest of his or her life.

Fr. Serra's desire was to make sure that the Indians had a steady food supply, so he taught them to raise crops and animals. He also made sure they learned building and smithing, weaving and sewing, as he had done with his parishioners in the Sierra Gorda. After the Indians were baptized, Fr. Serra required that they live near the Mission. This was for their own protection from warlike Indians and from renegade Spanish soldiers. Fr. Serra also knew that for the faith of the Indians to grow, they needed to live in a Catholic environment, and close proximity to the Mission made this possible.

Soon the Mission was supporting itself. The Indians grew their own crops and live-stock, made their own metal implements, built their own homes, and made their own clothing. Fr. Serra believed that the land belonged to the Indians. He believed that the Mission system should exist for a generation or so, long enough for the Indians to learn the way of life of the Spanish. He taught them the skills of Spanish civilization so that they could take their place as equals in the Spanish society that was sure to come to California.

The last thing he wanted was for the Indians to be deprived of their land or mistreated by the Spanish. He believed that the Mission system was the best way to insure that this did not happen.

There were many difficulties with which Fr. Serra had to cope. Soldiers had to ac-company each Mission to guard against Indian attack. The commanders of these soldiers, first Commandante Fages and then later Commandante Riviera, did all they could to make Fr. Serra's job as difficult as possible. They would often refuse permission for soldiers to accompany Fr. Serra to found a new Mission, and since he was not safe without soldiers at a new Mission site, Fr. Serra often had to wait for weeks or even many months before the commandante changed his mind.

Commandante Fages would not feed his soldiers with the food that had come by ship, forcing them to hunt and gather what they could themselves while he feasted on the food he denied his men. They were often starving.

When an Indian attacked a Mission and was later captured, Fr. Serra always urged com-passion. In this way, he turned enemies into friends. The Commandantes tried to punish these Indians severely, and went out of the way to take revenge on the whole tribe; Fr. Serra some-times was powerless to prevent this. The Commandantes sometimes let their men steal from and otherwise mistreat the Indians, and even let them dishonor Indian women without being punished for it. This caused many difficulties for the Indians and for Fr. Serra. He constantly stood up for what was right.

Commandante Fages heaped insult on injury when he accused Fr. Serra of not obeying the Commandante's authority and seeking too much power for himself. He refused to cooper-ate with the missionary effort. Fr. Serra had to journey to Mexico City to refute these accusa-tions; he was gone from the Missions for over a year. This trip turned out to be a blessing in disguise. He met with the Viceroy Buccarelli, and so impressed the Viceroy that he agreed to nearly all of Fr. Serra's requests. In this way, he gained the first "Bill of Rights" to protect the Indians and their interests in the New World. Viceroy Buccarelli became Fr. Serra's strongest ally and supporter, and his influence did much to heal the damage done to the missions by the Commandante.

The Spanish authorities permitted expeditions of Spanish settlers to travel to Upper California and make colonies there. Although Fr. Serra was a close friend of Colonel Anza, the leader of the first of these expeditions, in which he brought settlers to the San Francisco area in 1776, he was against the idea of Spanish settlements. He knew that the Indians needed more time – a generation or more – to learn the ways of Spanish civilization. To introduce Spanish settlers during the early years of the missions was to expose the Indians to vices that would undermine the new faith he was teaching them. Settlers would attract more settlers. These newcomers may try to cheat the Indians out of the land that was rightfully theirs. Settlers would be welcome after the Indians had settled and farmed the choicest land, Fr. Serra believed, not before.

There were other difficulties. Attack was common when a Mission was in its early years. The Indians attacked Mission San Diego and burned it to the ground. Fr. Luis Jalme, California's first martyr, was tortured and killed in the attack. He had used the customary greeting of the missions "Love God, my children," to the Indians who had come to attack the Mission. The Franciscans could hardly believe that one of their own had been martyred. They knew Fr. Jalme's deep commitment to serve the Indians, and continued teaching the Gospel to them and helping them in imitation of him. Fr. Serra felt sure that his prayers and sacrificial death helped their efforts.

Some of the Indians felt the lure of pagan life, and left the missions to return to the hills and forests to live as before. Some stole goods and even other Indian's wives before fleeing. Fr. Serra usually sent someone to find these Indians to try to persuade them to return. Some people accused Fr. Serra of keeping the Indians prisoner in his missions; this was not true. Only Indian maidens were locked in their quarters to protect them from dishonor from unruly Spanish soldiers. Others accused him of beating and enslaving the Indians; there is no evidence at all for this. Instead, Fr. Serra treated the Indians with compassion, and forgave wrongdoers. People who persisted in wrongdoing were punished by a slap on the wrist, which was a punishment common in Spanish lands that was intended to hurt the pride of the offender more than his wrist.

Fr. Serra never let any setbacks or problems discourage him. Neither assault by flaming arrows nor false accusations nor interference could keep him from putting his motto into practice: "Always go forward, never go back." What was his secret? He trusted completely in God's Providence, which is His constant loving care in the lives of each of His children.

"In all our labors, let us put our confidence in God. He is our Father. He knows what we need and that is enough," he said.

But triumphs were many, too. Fr. Serra and the Franciscans made great progress in attracting Indian converts to the Catholic faith. At the end of his life, Fr. Serra could count over five thousand Indians living as committed Catholics. They raised fourteen thousand head of livestock and harvested over seventeen thousand bushels of grain. They lived at or near nine missions served by twenty Franciscan priests.

Not all progress could be counted in numbers. Most wonderful of all to Fr. Serra was that so many Indian souls were full of God's grace, and gave glory to Him in their lives. He had a genuine affection for the Indians, and they returned this affection. To them, it was as though the love of Jesus were walking the earth again in the person of Fr. Serra. To him, it was as though the days of the early Church were repeated, in which people born to a pagan world became members of the Mystical Body of Christ.

It was always Fr. Serra's greatest desire to die as a martyr of the Catholic Faith. This was not to be. Worn out with overwork and suffering from tuberculosis, Fr. Serra made one last tour of the missions in 1783 and 1784. Holding the crucifix that went with him everywhere, he died in Mission San Carlos on August 28, 1784, and was buried in the chapel there.

What happened to the missions after the death of Fr. Serra? Unfortunately, the predictions of Fr. Serra came true. Twenty-one missions ranged the length of California, but the Mission system lasted only for about fifty years. Spanish settlements became numerous, and in a political move, the care of the missions was taken away from the Church. Not yet fully acclimated into Spanish culture and ways, the Indians were easy prey for exploitation. Unscrupulous Spanish settlers cheated the Indians out of the land which Fr. Serra wanted to remain in Indian hands, tricking them into selling it to them for far below its real value. Without the Franciscans to help them secure their best interests, the Indians fell into poverty and alcoholism, and were rapidly outnumbered by Spanish settlers.

The Mission buildings themselves fell into disrepair for a time, but gradually were repaired, and each of the nine founded by Fr. Serra is used as a church today. Fr. Serra is regarded as the Father of California and his statue is one of two from that state to grace the Rotunda of the Capitol in Washington, D. C. Fr. Serra has also been the inspiration for the organizations that do so much to promote religious vocations, called the Serra Clubs.

Bl. John Paul II beatified Fr. Serra on September 25, 1988. In paying him tribute, the Pope stated that Fr. Serra "sowed the seeds of Christian Faith amid the mountainous changes wrought by the arrival of European settlers in the New World. . . .In fulfilling this ministry, Father Serra showed himself to be a true son of St. Francis."

Lesson Activities
Bl. Junipero Serra

Vocabulary

Define the following.

sacrifice	apostolic	Providence	ideal
commitment	expedition	disembark	immensity
encroach	infection	rudiments	poultice
civilization	splendor		

Terms to Know

Discover the meaning of each of the following.

Franciscan

New World

Upper (Alta) California

Lower (Baja) California

Mystical Body of Christ

Comprehension Questions

Answer the following, using complete sentences.

1. What inspired Fr. Serra to bring the Christian Faith to the natives of the New World?

2. On the journey to Mexico City, Fr. Serra had a mishap. From what did he suffer for the rest of his life?

3. Although he himself lived an austere life, Fr. Serra believed in doing something with as much splendor as possible. What was it?

4. Give at least three examples of this.

5. When traveling back to San Fernando, Fr. Serra and a companion received kind hospitality from a small family who later disappeared. Later, whom did he realize they were?

6. Don José de Galvez became a good ally for Fr. Serra. What orders did he receive from Spain that were to change Fr. Serra's life?

7. What were two reasons for this?

8. On the trip to Upper California, Fr. Serra's leg was in a bad way. What made it better?

9. During the first year, setbacks were many at the San Diego Mission, but Fr. Serra was not discouraged at the lack of Indian converts. What did he write?

10. To the prayers of which saint did Fr. Serra credit the saving of the whole Mission to Upper California?

11. Fr. Serra's method for founding a Mission was simple. What two things did he do first?

12. What religious truths did Fr. Serra teach the Indians?

13. Name at least three work skills that Fr. Serra arranged for the Indians to learn.

14. Why did Fr. Serra teach the Indians the skills of Spanish civilization?

15. Fr. Serra's secret for success was to trust in God's Providence. Finish this quote of his: "In all our labors . . .

16. What was Fr. Serra's motto?

Analyze This

Using as many details as you can, explain each question in paragraph form.

1. Why did Miguel Serra become a priest?

2. How did Fr. Serra become a missionary?

3. How did he fight discouragement?

4. How did Fr. Serra deal with setbacks from others?

5. Why did he want to improve the lives of the Indians?

6. How did Fr. Serra succeed in improving the lives of the Indians?

7. Describe the steps Fr. Serra took to found a Mission.

8. What was important to Fr. Serra in the worship of God?

Essay Questions

Answer one or more of the following in essay form.

1. How did Fr. Serra's family influence his life for the good?

2. Describe Fr. Serra's priestly life before he arrived in the New World.

3. How was Fr. Serra a good influence on others?

4. How did Fr. Serra help others to worship God better?

5. Describe Fr. Serra's life in the Sierra Gorda.

6. What details were involved in founding a Mission?

7. Describe life in a California Mission.

8. What problems arose in the Mission system, and how did Fr. Serra deal with them?

9. Were Fr. Serra and his missions a success?

10. How does the life of Fr. Serra exemplify the saying of Jesus: "Whatsoever you do to the least of my brothers, you do unto Me"?

Quotes

Complete one or more of the following.

1. Select one or more quotations from Fr. Serra, memorize it/them, and recite it/them.

2. Choose a quote of Fr. Serra, and explain it in essay form. You may wish to give your composition as a speech.

Geography and History

Complete one or more of the following.

1. Draw and label a map of Mallorca and Spain.

2. Draw and label a map of the colonies of Spain in Fr. Serra's time.

3. Draw and label a map of Mexico, using the place names mentioned in the story.

4. Draw and label a map of Alta (Upper) California, and the missions Fr. Serra founded. You may wish to include the other missions that were founded by his successors.

5. List each Mission founded by Fr. Serra, and beside each one, list the city that grew

from it. Bonus: find out what were the original names of the cities of San Francisco and Los Angeles.

6. Write a brief report on the island of Mallorca.

7. Write a report on the colonization of Mexico.

8. Write a report on the colonial holdings of Spain throughout history.

9. Draw a diagram of the layout of one of Fr. Serra's missions.

10. Write a brief report of the swallows of San Juan Capistrano.

Research and Report

Choose one or more of the following topics, and research and write a report about it. Be sure to include related maps, diagrams, time lines, and illustrations.

1. Baja (Lower) California

2. The History of the Indians of the State of California

3. The History of the State of California

4. The History of one of Fr. Serra's Missions (choose one.)

5. The History of Mexico City

6. Our Lady of Guadalupe and Her Influence on the New World

7. Franciscan Missions and Missionaries

You, The Biographer

Research and write a biography of one or more persons listed below. Be sure to use at least two sources for your biography. You may wish to present it as a speech.

1. Choose one of Fr. Serra's missions, and discover which saint it is named after. Then, research and write a biography of that saint.

2. Colonel Anza

3. Fr. Luis Jalme

4. St. Francis of Assisi

Putting Your Faith into Practice

Choose one or more of the following.

1. How has the example of Fr. Serra helped you to live a more dedicated Christian life?

2. Dealing with a chronic disease or impairment like Fr. Serra did is never easy. Perhaps you know of someone who "carries on" with life despite the inconvenience or pain of such a disease or impairment. Interview them, and ask one or more of the following questions: How important is your Christian faith to you? What part does it play in helping you cope with your difficulty? What do you do to deal with discouragement? How has your difficulty made you more compassionate toward others?

3. The plight of American Indians is often a difficult one. There are missionaries in this country who serve the Indians materially and spiritually. Find out all you can about one such missionary group and the Indians they serve. Earn some money, and send it to them. Keep in contact with them, and try somehow to contribute regularly.

4. Unfortunately, anti-Catholicism is alive and well in our country. Bl. Junipero Serra has been the subject of accusations of cruelty that are completely untrue by people who want to believe that the Church is always harmful and that the best thing for us all is that we all return to paganism. As a Catholic, you will meet people who oppose the Catholic faith. What can you do to make your faith stronger, and what can you do to be prepared to refute their arguments? Read a book on Catholic Apologetics, and develop a plan for your life to safeguard your faith so that it can grow stronger.

5. Fr. Serra had a great trust in the Providence of God. How have you seen the hand of God guiding you in the events of your life? How has a seemingly "chance" event changed your life? Write your reflections on this. How can you be an instrument of the Providence of God in the lives of others?

6. There is an old saying: "We must pray as if all depended on God, and work as though all depended on ourselves." How does the life of Fr. Serra exemplify this saying? How can you, using the lessons of Fr. Serra's life, put this saying to good use in your own life? Write an essay or make a speech on this.

7. Fr. Serra is known as the Father of the State of California. He had no desire at all for such an honor; he only wanted to bring God to the Indians. How have good actions resulted in unexpectedly better results in other events of history and in your own life?

St. Teresa Benedicta of the Cross

Blessed by the Truth

Echt, Holland
Sunday, August 2, 1942

It was a quiet summer afternoon at the Carmelite Monastery in Echt. The sisters of Carmel had relaxed duties, as they always did on Sunday. Clad in their brown habits, they went about their different pursuits. Some studied, some tended plants, others prayed, others did hand work.

One sister sat at a desk covered with books and papers. She was writing a book herself, one on St. John of the Cross, the Spanish master of prayer and co-founder of her Discalced Carmelite Order. As usual, she was completely absorbed in her work. Her book was called *The Science of the Cross*, and in it she wrote about the spiritual life seen in the light of eternity and the Cross of Christ. This sister was Edith Stein. In Carmel, as was the custom, she had taken a new name: Sr. Teresa Blessed by the Cross.

It was nearly five o'clock. Edith knew that before long it would be time for the sisters to gather in the church and pray the Divine Office. This was their main purpose. Seven times a day they gathered to pray psalms and canticles for the needs of the Church and the conversion of sinners. Their prayer called God's grace down on everyone. Some said that it even upheld the world.

Edith smiled as she wrote about St. John's death. As the saint lay dying, his brothers in religion saw a bright light in his room as they prayed.

"It shone like the sun and the moon…," said a witness. Then the brothers noticed that "the saint … was without life." "Our Father has gone to heaven in this light," said one. Such a wonderful holy death, she thought to herself.

A footfall sounded in the doorway. Edith looked up and saw Sr. Antonia, her superior, smile at her.

"Sister Teresa, the SS officers are here and they want to speak to you," she said. "They are waiting in the parlor. Perhaps they are here to discuss your emigration status."

"Let's hope they have some good news," replied Edith with a smile. She lay down her pen and rose from her chair. Walking to the parlor, she wondered if the Nazi German occupation forces would give her permission to emigrate to Switzerland.

Edith Stein was a Jew. She had been an atheist for much of her life until she converted and entered the Catholic Church at age thirty. Nine years ago, at age forty-two, she entered Carmel as a sister. None of this mattered to the Nazis. They rounded up all Jews, confined them to work camps, forced them to work, to contribute to the war effort, and executed them. Since there were more Jewish people than slave labor jobs, the Nazis began to execute their prisoners soon after capture. Most Jews did not know what awaited them.

The Dutch Catholic bishops knew that innocent men, women, and children were being unfairly deported and imprisoned. They had no armies to prevent this, but they had the Mystical Body of Christ. They composed a protest letter and appeal for prayer, and this letter had been read at Sunday Mass in every parish in Holland the previous Sunday. Optimists hoped that the Nazis would now stop rounding up Jews, but realists knew the Nazi habit of revenge and feared the worst.

Edith and her sister Rosa, also a Catholic convert, were trying to emigrate to Switzerland, which was a neutral country. They had already escaped Germany and come to Holland, but the Germans then marched in and occupied Holland, too. Awaiting word, Rosa helped at the Carmel and Edith wrote. Would today bring the permission they needed?

Edith walked into the monastery parlor. It was a room divided in two by a grille. The grille was there not to keep the nuns inside, but to keep the world outside so that they could devote themselves more completely to prayer. Behind the grille stood two SS officers. They weren't smiling.

"Step away from the grille!" One of them shouted. Edith's friendly smile faded. She backed up a few paces.

"You have only five minutes to pack your belongings!" shouted the officer. "Then you are to come with us!"

Edith stood there, stunned. She turned to see Sr. Antonia step up to the grille, pale with shock.

"There must be some mistake," she began. Edith heard Sr. Antonia's soft voice attempt to bargain with the harsh voices of the soldiers as she walked slowly down the hall to her room. Word traveled fast. Some sisters were already packing for her, their faces stunned. Edith seemed to recover from her shock.

"Pray for me, sisters. Pray for me and my sister, Rosa," she said. Gathering around her as if to give her strength, they assured her that they would.

"Contact the Swiss Consulate again. Maybe they can help," she added. Perhaps Edith was trying to console the sisters by giving them something to hope for. In her eyes was sorrow mixed with resignation and courage. She accepted the inevitable.

Edith walked outside to the convent gate where the Nazis and a frightened Rosa were awaiting her. It did not matter to the Nazis that Edith was a doctor of philosophy and a college instructor, one of the first women in Germany to have achieved this. It did not matter that Edith was a world-renowned philosopher and writer in her own right, or that she had lectured on current problems and their solutions to large crowds. All that mattered to the Nazis was that Edith was a Jew. For this they were taking her away.

Edith and Rosa turned to the sisters for a last farewell. The street outside the gate began to fill up with people of the neighborhood who had heard what was happening. They were angry at the Nazi action, and their angry murmurs grew to angry shouts.

Edith turned to Rosa, who was surrounded by the crowd. She looked utterly bewildered, as if she could not take in what was happening to them. Edith took Rosa's hand and held it in hers.

"Come, Rosa. We are going for our people," Edith said to her sister.

Edith accepted her coming death and offered it for the Jewish people. She and Rosa walked together to the corner where a car awaited them. They got into the car. It sped the sisters away.

*   *   *

Who was Edith Stein?

She was born on the Jewish Day of Atonement on October 12, 1891. All her life she regarded the day of her birth as significant. The Day of Atonement, also known as Yom Kipper, is a day of special prayer and repentance. Devout Jews fast from food and water on this day, and spend many hours in the synagogue to make amends to God and to ask for His blessings.

Edith was the youngest of seven surviving children in a very devout Jewish family. She grew up practicing the Jewish faith. The family celebrated all the major Jewish holidays, such as Passover, Yom Kippur, and Jewish New Year. To usher in each Sabbath, the lady of the house would light special candles and call down God's blessings upon her family who stood around her at prayerful attention.

Edith's mother was wise and intelligent. Her father was hardworking and kind. They taught their children to honor and help the poor, to dedicate first fruits to God, to do their best in work and study, and to help all in need. These values took deep root in Edith from her earliest years.

One day, when Edith was almost two years old, she watched her father get ready for a business trip. He owned and ran a lumber business, so trips were a regular thing. Edith hugged and kissed him goodbye, then watched as he walked out of the house. Standing at the doorway, she called him back for another goodbye. Smiling good-naturedly, he came! Edith hugged and kissed her beloved father a second time.

Not long afterward, the family heard some terrible news: Herr Stein collapsed and died of a stroke! The happy family was devastated. They all remembered how Edith had called her father back for a second goodbye, as if she knew that something would happen to him. Frau Stein took over running the lumber business, and the older children took care of the younger.

Frau Stein had no easy task ahead of her when she took over the family lumber business. The business was ridden with debts. Frau Stein came from a long line of business owners, so the daily demands of the business world were not new to her, but the lumber business was. She knew little about it, so she determined to learn all she needed to know. In a short time, she was

Edith Stein's family. The young girl seated in front is Edith at approximately 3 years old.

able to handle customers and their lumber specifications with ease.

At first, the entire family lived in an apartment of only three rooms. Money was scarce, and the family learned to "make do" with little, and to make things last. Edith never felt the sting of poverty as a child because she was grateful for whatever she had. Frau Stein had strict standards of housekeeping, which all her children followed; everything was clean and neat, and visitors were amazed that a small apartment could look so fine and elegant. Frau Stein worked diligently to bring the business out of debt. Soon she was running a prosperous business, and moved the family to a roomy home. Edith was grateful for the lessons of thrift and used them all her life.

Edith loved the family business because she could play in the lumberyard all she wanted. The Stein lumberyard was also a favorite playground for the children of the neighborhood. Edith remembered many happy hours spent playing hide-and-seek in the fresh air. Edith regarded such a place as an important part of childhood because all children need places to meet, to play, to create games and plays, to prove themselves, and to exercise.

The employees of the lumberyard were treated with all the kindness given to actual members of the family. Frau Stein even took care of them when they became ill. Many times Edith would get a wood sliver in her hand, and any of these workers gladly would pull it out for her.

As a small child, Edith had a strong temper and a will of iron. She wanted to go to school at age six, and she even told her mother that she was willing to forego any birthday presents if only she could go to school! Her mother consented. Edith considered kindergarten to be beneath her dignity, so she started in regular school several months late. She rapidly caught up, and became the best student in the class. She would hold this position all throughout her school years. Her mother was fond of saying, "It is not enough for Jews to be as good as others – they must be better." Edith took this advice to heart.

Edith loved school. "In school, people took me seriously," she remembered. She was no longer the youngest and smallest, as she was in her family. But at age seven, the lively little girl became introverted and lonely. Edith began to think deeply about things. She felt deeply, too; the sight of a drunken person on the street, for example, moved her to tears. Her compassion for suffering grew. Edith learned to be a self-controlled person so that her weaknesses would not take over and rule her. In this way, she achieved true freedom of spirit. She read constantly, even when her older sister brushed and arranged her hair. Edith ceaselessly sought the truth.

When Edith was thirteen, she had a painful experience of anti-Semitism, or prejudice against Jews. Edith was her school's most accomplished student. Everyone expected her to win the school award for highest excellence in academics. But when it came time to award the prize, school officials gave it to someone else – someone who was not a Jew!

Her classmates were stunned and saddened, Edith most of all. They all knew that Edith was passed over for the award only because she was a Jew. The injustice hurt her. Soon afterward, she made to her mother a surprising request. Edith wanted to quit school.

Even more surprisingly her mother agreed. This was not because Frau Stein valued school little. On the contrary, all of the Stein brothers and sisters became educated and accomplished adults. Rather, it was because she could see that Edith needed the break in order to work things out for herself.

Edith stayed with her older sister, Else, for 8 months and helped take care of her children. Edith also stopped believing in God, and became an atheist. Perhaps this was a reaction to the injustice done to her. Edith wanted to be independent of everyone, including God, so that she could be truly free. But in asserting her freedom, she left behind God, the source of truth and freedom. So she began to seek "the truth" in her studies.

At her mother's prompting, Edith returned to school willingly. Her goal was to be a teacher. She took up the study of Latin; she came to love the language because of its elegance and its regular rules. She grew to be sociable and more animated. Edith had lots of friends, and at age 17 she began to tutor some of her fellow students for the sheer joy of teaching.

She loved taking walks amid the beauties of nature. Despite the long skirts and high collars of the time, Edith and her friends loved going hiking in the mountains and canoeing in the rivers. Edith played tennis, and became renowned as a skilled and graceful dancer. And, as always, she sought the truth.

For Edith, truth was not just an abstract idea, but was "incarnated in persons," and inseparable from love. What was life? How do we know something is true? What will help me find the truth? These questions always were with Edith.

Even though she was successful in her studies, Edith suffered through periods of depression. Perhaps she was tempted to despair of ever finding the truth. She made the mistake of reading a book that described the bad side of life, and Edith was shocked to discover so much evil. When she was rescued from a potentially fatal gas leak, she was disappointed that she did not die. She tried to pull herself out of despair; attending a festival of Bach's music, she came out of her depression.

At age 20 she took her comprehensive examinations and attended the university. She studied psychology but gave it up because it was not precise and scientific enough for her. She took up the study of philosophy, or the pursuit of wisdom through the search for basic principles. In this exacting course of study, Edith excelled.

She became interested in phenomenology, the method of arriving at absolute essences through the analysis of living experience. Edith saw phenomenology as a philosophical tool to find the truth.

She studied under the phenomenologist philosopher Edmund Husserl. Husserl taught

Edith with friends (she is at the top in the back.)

that truth does not change but endures eternally; it is necessary and knowable by every mind. This was welcome news for Edith, who did not believe the philosophers who said that all we can know about is our own thoughts. According to such philosophers, two people could not truly discuss any shared experience or idea, because each person had different thoughts in his/her mind about it, and could only report what his/her ideas were.

Edith knew this was untrue. People seek to connect with one another and such a philosophy would prohibit any true communication. It would also mean that truth was unknowable. Edith eagerly studied phenomenology because it held that truth was knowable.

Thinking about this time in her life years later, Edith said simply, "My search for the truth was a constant prayer."

She studied at the University of Gottingen where, it was said, everyone discusses philosophy all day long! Edith loved to discuss different philosophies with her friends and fellow students; classrooms, cafes, and long walks in the country were all good places for that. Edith made many friends during her university years; Hedwig Martius, Theodore Conrad, Adolf and Anna Reinach, and Hans Lipps all were good friends of hers. She had a real gift for friendship, and kept in touch with friends by letter and visits all her life.

Edith began work on her dissertation, entitling it "On the Problem of Empathy." She ran into difficulties, and had a hard time writing it. Edith fell into another deep depression. She sought out Adolf Reinach, a fellow phenomenologist and leader of Husserl's students. He listened to her, and gave her kind, constructive advice. Edith felt better immediately, and continued to work on her dissertation.

During this time, World War I broke out. One by one, Edith's friends volunteered to fight or to serve. Many were the casualties in this terrible war. In 1915, Edith too felt compelled to serve. Her mother was shocked, and forbade her to go.

"Then I must do so without your consent," replied Edith.

"I have no private life any more. All my energy must be devoted to this great happening. Only when the war is over, if I'm alive then, will I be permitted to think of my private affairs once again," said Edith. She served as a volunteer nurse with the Red Cross. She nursed Austrian soldiers who were under care for such diseases as cholera, dysentery, and typhus, as well as those injured by bullets and shrapnel. Edith carried out her nursing duties in her usual energetic way. She assisted doctors who operated on the soldiers' wounds, handing them the surgical instruments they needed; Edith watched the surgeries carefully, and became good at anticipating which instrument the doctor would want next. She bathed and bandaged, cleaned and comforted. Edith came into contact with many different people from many different countries, backgrounds, and cultures. She was able to get along well with everyone, even people whom others considered difficult. It edified her, when she saw how the injured soldiers were grateful for the smallest favors.

Even though the war continued, Edith returned to her studies. She followed Dr. Husserl to the University of Friborg, and became his assistant in 1916. She visited Frankfort to see some famous monuments and works of art. Edith had a memorable experience when she visited the Cathedral in Frankfort:

"We went into the Cathedral for a few moments, and as we stood there in respectful silence, a woman came in with her shopping basket and knelt down in one of the pews to say a short prayer. That was something completely new to me. In the synagogue, as in the Protestant churches I had visited, people only went in at the time of the service. But here was someone coming into the empty church in the middle of a day's work as if to talk with a friend. I have never been able to forget that day."

Edith began to see that the life of faith was not so much the acceptance of an idea as it was a relationship with a Person.

She continued working hard on her dissertation for her doctoral degree and finally finished it. Edith received her doctorate in philosophy in 1917. She was now Fraulein Doctor Edith Stein.

At the end of that year, Edith had an experience that would change the course of her life. She was a close friend of Adolf Reinach and his wife Anna. Edith received word that Reinach was killed in action at Flanders. Edith herself was devastated at the loss of such a good friend; Reinach had gathered young philosophers around himself with such ease. Edith didn't know how she and her friends could cope with such a loss. She knew that Reinach and his wife were Christians. Still, she couldn't imagine what Anna Reinach must have been going through. Edith decided to pay her a condolence visit.

Expecting to find a woman broken with sorrow, Edith was surprised to find that Anna Reinach was full of hope and peace! She moved among her visitors and consoled them. Edith was thunderstruck. From Anna Reinach shone the light of faith. Edith had never seen such a thing before. Late in life, she wrote about this event.

"It was my first encounter with the Cross and the divine power that it bestows on those who carry it. For the first time, I was seeing with my very eyes the Church, born from its Redeemer's sufferings, triumphant over the sting of death. That was the moment my unbelief collapsed and Christ shone forth – in the mystery of the Cross."

For Edith, it was like a glimpse into another world – the world of faith. Anna Reinach had experienced the Cross in the loss of her beloved husband, and the Cross gave her light and peace. Edith wanted to join this world, and struggled with how to do this for the next several years. She read the New Testament and visited churches.

The war ended in 1918 with Germany defeated; the mood in the country was somber. So Edith was not surprised when her application to be a university professor was turned town. She returned to her home in Breslau, continued her research, and tutored students privately.

In the summer of 1921 she stayed with her friend Hedwig Conrad-Martius and her husband, Theodore Conrad, at their farmhouse. Hedwig and Theodore farmed an orchard and garden by day and philosophized by night. They graciously welcomed fellow philosophers as their guests, and Edith had stayed with them often. The couple had to go out one evening, leaving Edith alone in the big house. Finding herself in their library, she selected a book to read: _The Life of Teresa of Jesus_, which was the autobiography of the great Spanish Carmelite saint. Taking it with her, Edith found a comfortable place and began to read.

She read all night long. She did not stop until she finished the whole book. Closing the book, she said, "This is the truth." Edith realized that knowledge took her only so far, and also realized that God gives Himself to the heart that surrenders to Him. In St. Teresa's autobiography, Edith could see the saint struggling to find God Who Himself was searching for her all along. She became devoted to St. Teresa; an added delight to her was that St. Teresa and her good friend St. John of the Cross were said to have Jewish ancestors!

Edith bought herself a catechism and a missal and studied them both. She attended her first Mass, and afterward asked the priest to baptize her! The surprised priest examined her and found that she had taught herself about the Catholic Faith surprisingly well. Edith was baptized on January 1, 1922, taking the name Teresa in honor of St. Teresa of Avila and Hedwig in honor of her friend. Hedwig Conrad-Martius was her sponsor, and Edith wore Hedwig's wedding dress as her baptismal dress. From this day forward Edith wanted to be a Carmelite nun. She was confirmed on February 2nd, and began a lifelong practice of attending daily Mass. She knew that her commitment to Christ had to be a complete one, so she decided never to marry.

When Edith told her family that she had become a Catholic, they were very unhappy; for the first time Edith saw her mother cry. Frau Stein was devastated. Edith offered this suffering to God in union with the Cross of Christ. Edith continued to accompany her mother to the synagogue whenever she visited home, and even her mother was impressed with how Edith prayed there. "I have never seen anyone pray like Edith," an amazed Frau Stein said later.

Edith took a job at St. Magdalena, a high school for girls and a teacher's college run by Dominican sisters, in Speyer. She taught the girls and the teachers-in-training for seven years, and sometimes even taught the sisters. Edith could have taken a job at a prestigious university.

But she knew that she needed to be in a Catholic environment for her faith to grow. This is why she chose St. Magdalena in which to live and work.

Edith was a person short of stature with expressive dark eyes. In the memories of the girls and young women she taught, as well as those of the Dominican Sisters who ran St. Magdalena, she was one of the most influential persons in their lives. She influenced them by her example. One student remembered that Edith brought into perfect harmony a life of prayer with a life of action. She dressed plainly, and refused any surplus salary. She was happy to give extra help to any student who asked for it, and was a warm friend to anyone with personal problems or who suffered from homesickness. Edith often visited poor people in the town, taking packages to them. Since her days were so full, Edith would often spend most of the night praying before the Blessed Sacrament in the chapel. She had a favorite seat and kneeled behind a pillar of the church where she could see the altar and Tabernacle without being seen, and she loved to spend time with Our Lord there. When asked what gave her strength for her busy days, Edith answered that it was prayer.

Edith loved the Mass. She followed the liturgical year with close attention. Edith wanted to live the life of Christ through the liturgical year at Mass and, in so doing, become more united to Him. Attending daily, she sat up front so she could concentrate completely on the Holy Sacrifice of the Mass without any distractions. Many witnesses were impressed with Edith's complete concentration at Mass, and strove to follow her example. She spent many vacations at the Benedictine Abbey at Beuron, receiving spiritual direction there.

In addition to her teaching duties at St. Magdalena, Edith wrote letters to her many friends, and went on several lecture tours. She translated and wrote about the works of St. Thomas Aquinas, one of the world's greatest philosophers. In 1931 she left St. Magdalena to finish this project, and later took a lectureship at the Educational Institute in Munster in order to reform the educational system. Giving speeches to teachers' organizations, women's groups, and academic organizations, Edith was kept busy. She even spoke on the radio.

She witnessed Jews being publicly attacked, and was horrified at this. Edith seems to have realized before others did what the agenda of the Nazis really was, and she wrote to the Pope to warn him that the Nazis meant to execute the Jews as a people. Unfortunately the two could not meet, but the Pope kept her letter. He sent her a warm letter in return, conveying blessings on her and her family. He died not long after, and the new Pope incorporated some of her letter into his teachings. This Pope, Pius XII, used every means possible to save the Jews of Europe. He was responsible for saving over 800,000 Jews from death during the war. The head rabbi of Rome, Israel Zolli, was so impressed with the Pope's tireless efforts to save Jews that he himself became a Catholic, taking the Pope's first name of Eugenio as his own confirmation name in the Pope's honor!

All Edith wanted to do since her conversion was to be a Carmelite nun. Since she was such an educated, renowned teacher, she was advised to serve God as a professor. This she did until it became clear that Jews would be forced out of all professional positions. Edith volunteered to take up this Cross on behalf of and in union with the Jewish people. A school

in South America offered Edith a job that would allow her to finish her book on St. Thomas Aquinas. Having many choices before her made making a decision very difficult for Edith. She struggled a great deal. Finally, putting herself in the hands of God, Edith decided to enter Carmel. This put her at peace.

Her peace would not last long, but it would be replaced by the darkness of faith. This was because Edith had to tell her family about her decision. One Sunday in September, Edith sat with her mother who sat knitting near a window. Finally her mother spoke.

"What are you going to do in Cologne with the nuns?" she asked Edith.

"Live with them," answered Edith. She later said that this was the moment where "peace left the family." Her mother was always polite, but she simply could not understand Edith's decision.

"I don't want to have anything against Jesus," Frau Stein would say. "He may have been a very good person. But why did he have to make himself God?" Edith knew that the time was not right to answer her mother's questions, and maintained a charitable silence.

Edith accompanied her mother to the synagogue for the last time. Many people came to the house that day to wish Edith well. After the crowds of people left, Frau Stein put her face in her hands and began to cry. Edith embraced her for a long time. Both women went to bed, but neither got any sleep.

Three days later, on October 15, 1933, Edith entered the Carmel of Cologne, Germany. It was no accident that she entered Carmel on the Feast of St. Teresa of Avila. Her acceptance ceremony as a novice took place on April 15, 1934. She wore a white silk wedding dress that was later made into a priest's chasuble. This custom was appropriate because a Carmelite's purpose is to pray for priests, for the needs of the church, and for the conversion of sinners.

As was the Carmelite custom, Edith took a new name: Sister Teresa Benedicta a Cruce. Edith loved St. Benedict, and had been devoted to the Cross since her conversion; one way of rendering her name is Sr. Teresa Benedicta of the Cross. But her name had a second meaning, a meaning on which she was to pray and meditate for the rest of her life: Sr. Teresa Blessed by the Cross. She continued to identify with the sufferings of the Jewish people.

Commenting on her name, she said, "By the Cross, I understood the fate of the people of God, which was then already beginning to be proclaimed." Finally, Edith was happy and at peace.

How did Edith strive to live out her vocation as a Carmelite?

Writing to a Jewish friend to explain Carmel, Edith said, "Whoever enters Carmel is not lost to her own, but is theirs fully for the first time; it is our vocation to stand before God for all." Carmelites pray seven times a day for the needs of everyone.

"Only the person who renounces self-importance, who no longer struggles to defend or assert himself, can be large enough for God's boundless action," she wrote later. She wished to be completely humble so that she could freely receive the grace of God. She said to the Mother Prioress of Carmel: "It is not human activity that can help us, but the sufferings of Christ. I aspire to share them." What an extraordinary statement from a woman who excelled at balancing faith and action! Knowing that she could do all things through Jesus, Who strengthened her, Edith put complete trust in Him. She made her first vows on Easter of 1935. As was Carmelite custom, she wore a crown of white roses.

Housework duties are as much a part of a Carmelite nun's day as is her round of prayer. Edith was terrible at housework. She freely acknowledged this, and humbly and cheerfully begged the community's pardon for each thing she broke or ruined! Always she kept trying.

What Edith loved best about Carmel was her closeness to Jesus, her Spouse in the Blessed Sacrament.

Edith corresponded with her many friends and relatives by letter. Jewish friends preparing to emigrate wrote or visited her for advice. Her mother was ailing, and Edith asked her friends to pray for her. Her sister Rosa wanted to become Catholic, but dared not enter the Church yet for fear of further devastating their mother. Edith prayed for Rosa and encouraged her.

On September 14, 1936, the Feast of the Holy Cross, Edith renewed her vows. At the very same moment that Edith joyfully pronounced the words renewing her vows, she was surprised by the strong sense that her mother was standing beside her. Soon afterward, Edith received a telegram telling her of the day and time of her mother's death; Frau Stein died the very moment that her daughter renewed her vows.

The next winter, Edith fell down a flight of stairs and broke a wrist and ankle. She had to visit a hospital outside her Carmel to have these treated. This misfortune led to an unusual blessing. While outside of Carmel, Edith was able to be present for her sister Rosa's baptism into the Catholic Church!

Terrible things were happening to Jews in Germany. On the night of November 8-9, 1938, Nazi SS troops smashed Jewish homes, businesses, and synagogues. This violent night became known as Kristallnacht, or "crystal night," because so many windows were broken in Jewish synagogues, homes, and businesses. Now it was too dangerous to be a Jew in Germany. Shortly thereafter, Edith's prioress tried to make arrangements for Edith to move to the Carmel in Bethlehem. Edith loved the fact that she, as a Jew, was related to Jesus by blood ties. To live in the Holy Land would be happiness indeed. Unfortunately, these plans did not work out. So instead, Edith moved to the Carmel in Echt, Holland, on New Year's Eve 1938.

Edith missed all her sisters from the Cologne Carmel very much. The sisters in her new home at Echt welcomed her warmly, and soon she felt at home. Edith offered herself, her life,

Convent enclosure chapel where Edith prayed

and her sufferings for the Jewish people, for the averting of war, and for the sanctification of her Carmelite family. Like Queen Esther, Edith interceded for all.

In 1940 Rosa came to live with her at the Echt Carmel. This was pure joy for Edith. The Stein sisters were happy and grateful to be together. Although not a nun, Rosa found many ways to be of help, and she was given the duty of doorkeeper for the monastery. The sisters and the townspeople quickly grew fond of her.

Later this same year, the Nazis occupied Holland. Edith suffered greatly at what was happening to innocent people under Nazi occupation, especially to Jews. The Nazis were waging war on more and more countries. So much suffering, thought Edith. She looked often at her two favorite pictures: the face of Christ on the Shroud of Turin, and the drawing of Jesus Crucified done by St. John of the Cross. With each moment of looking at these holy images, Edith offered herself in union with the sufferings of Christ for the salvation of all.

When she had been a teacher, Edith had written about philosophy, current problems, the important role of women, and education. Now she wrote for the Church as its loving daughter.

Time and time again, she returns to the theme of prayer:

"Every true prayer is a prayer of the Church, every true prayer had repercussions within the Church, and every true prayer is, ultimately, prayed by the Church, since it is the Church's indwelling Holy Spirit that prays within each individual 'with sighs too deep for words' (Romans 8:26).

That is the mark of all true prayer 'for no one can say that Jesus is Lord except in the Holy Spirit.' (1 Corinthians 12:3)"

The centenary of St. John of the Cross would be in 1942. To commemorate this occasion, Edith's superior Sr. Antonia asked Edith to write a book on this great Carmelite saint. She excused Edith from housework, and Edith joyfully set to work on _The Science of the Cross_.

Edith attempted to understand St. John of the Cross "through the unity of his being as it is expressed in his life and works…" The book is a biography, a philosophical work, a psychological study, and a treatise on prayer, all at the same time. It is also a masterpiece.

By 1942, Edith realized that she was putting her Carmel in danger by being there. Jews were being arrested every day, as were also people hiding and helping them. Edith applied for permission to emigrate to a Carmel in Switzerland. She kept writing.

Catholic and Protestant leaders protested the mass deportation of the Jews. The Bishops of Holland wrote a pastoral letter calling for an end to this, and calling for prayer and Christian action. The Nazis retaliated by arresting even more Jews. Edith and Rosa were among them.

The prisoners were taken to a camp called Amersfoort. Edith and Rosa discovered fifteen other religious – priests, brothers, and sisters – at the camp. This group clustered around Edith, and together they recited the Divine Office and the Rosary. The religious did all they could to help the hundreds of men, women, and children who were their fellow prisoners. One witness said of Edith: "The influence she exerted by her tranquil bearing and manner was undeniable."

Next, the prisoners were taken to a camp called Westerbork. Hours were spent filling out useless forms. Married couples were forever separated. It was a living nightmare. Prisoners were photographed with their prison I.D. number, then herded into barracks that lacked even the necessities of living.

Many women became severely depressed, moaning and staring into space for hours or days on end. Some were nearly insane with anxiety, and paid no attention to the needs of their children. It was Edith who cared for these children. She washed and tidied them, combed their hair, fed and cared for them. Witnesses who survived described Edith as "like an angel, comforting, helping, and consoling…" Although she was middle-aged and had some gray in her hair, she seemed "so young … so whole and honest and genuine."

Camp authorities allowed Edith to write to the convent for supplies. Eagerly the sisters assembled blankets, medicines, and other supplies. Two townsmen from Echt volunteered to deliver them to the camp.

Some kind Dutch police allowed the men to meet with Edith and Rosa at the camp. Edith's quiet, calm, almost cheerful demeanor struck them. She thanked them for the supplies and described camp life to the men as they stood smoking. Jokingly they offered her a cigarette, which made her laugh. She told them that she had tried smoking years ago when she was a university student. Telling them that she and Rosa would probably be sent to Silesia to work in the mines, Edith said that their first priority would always be prayer. As the whistle blew that signaled the prisoners to return to the barracks, Edith told them not to worry about the prisoners – they were "in God's hands." They bade one another farewell.

Prisoners were awakened in the middle of the night of August 7. They assembled and stood at attention to listen to the list of names being read aloud of all the prisoners to be deported. Each name was painful to hear. As dawn rose, the prisoners walked in a long line to the train with the Nazi SS as their guards. Only a handful of prisoners remained. These waved farewell to the vast crowd on the train. Edith and Rosa rode east.

That same day, Edith's train pulled into the station at Schifferstadt. Edith called to the stationmaster, who was on the platform.

"Do you know the family of Dean Schwind?"

"Yes, we were classmates. The Dean was here on the platform just a few minutes ago!" he replied.

"Please, sir, convey Edith Stein's greetings to the Dean and his family, and let them know that I am on my way to the east," said Edith. The stationmaster nodded, and the train began to pull out. He watched the train until it was out of sight. It was the last time Edith was seen alive.

Edith and Rosa reached Auschwitz on or about August 9, 1942. All prisoners on her train were ushered off the train and killed immediately after arrival by poison gas, their remains burned by the camp crematoria. How beautiful the sight of eternity must have been to Edith, whose eyes had seen so much suffering.

Edith wrote a beautiful prayer that sums up her relationship with God:

"Lord, let me walk without seeing on the paths that are Yours. I do not want to know where You are leading me. Am I not Your child? You are the Father of Wisdom and also my Father. Even if You lead me through the night, it is towards You. Lord, let happen what You will - I am ready, even if you do not satisfy my desire in this life. You are the Lord of Time. Do everything according to the plans of Your Wisdom. When You call gently to sacrifice, help me, yes, to perform it. Allow me to go completely beyond my little 'me,' so that, dead to myself, I might live only for You!"

St. Teresa Benedicta of the Cross was canonized a saint of the Catholic Church by Bl. John Paul II on October 11, 1998.

Drawing of Christ crucified originally by St. John of the Cross, redrawn by St. Edith Stein.

Lesson Activities
St. Edith Stein

Vocabulary

Define the following.

conversion	philosophy	incarnate	Carmelite
grace	atonement	phenomenology	correspond
resignation	introvert	missal	deportation
compassion	eternal	endure	dissertation
condolence	autobiography	liturgy	vocation

Terms to Know

Discover the meaning of each of the following.

Mystical Body of Christ

Holocaust

Liturgical Year

Comprehension Questions

Answer the following, using complete sentences.

1. Edith Stein was a Carmelite nun. What is the main purpose of Carmelite nuns?

2. What did Edith say to her sister when the Nazi SS ["Schutzstaffel" – Protective Squadron] took them prisoner?

3. What values taught by her devout Jewish parents took deep root in Edith?

4. Edith was passed over for an academic award because she was Jewish. What effect did this injustice have on her?

5. In college, Edith studied phenomenology because she saw it as a tool to find the truth. What is phenomenology?

6. Edith was devastated at the death of her friend Adolf Reinach. When she paid her friend, Anna Reinach, a condolence visit, what did she expect to find, and what did she find instead?

7. While staying with friends, Edith stayed up all night reading *The Life of Teresa of Jesus*. This experience led her directly to join the Catholic Church. What did Edith say when she finished the book?

8. Edith taught at St. Magdalena for seven years. Why did she choose to teach here rather than at a prestigious university?

9. When she entered Carmel, Edith told Mother Prioress: "It is not human activity that can help us…" Please finish this quote.

10. Soon after a night of Nazi violence against the Jews, Edith moved to the Carmel of Echt, Holland. What do historians call this night, and why?

11. Catholic bishops and priests in Holland protested the deportation of the Jews by the Nazis. Did this make the Nazis stop?

12. Many women prisoners were so depressed that they neglected their children. What did Edith do?

Analyze This

Using as many details as you can, explain each question in paragraph form.

1. Why did Edith Stein become an atheist?

2. What brought Edith into the Catholic Church?

3. How did Edith cope with Nazi persecution?

4. What attracted Edith to Carmel?

5. How did Edith live out her vocation in Carmel?

6. How did Edith see herself in solidarity with the Jewish people?

Essay Questions

Answer one or more of the following in essay form.

1. What values does the life of Edith Stein exemplify?

2. What could have motivated the Nazis to persecute the Jews, and why is evil always an "easy way"?

3. What strategies did Edith use in order to cope with the persecution of the Jews?

4. Explain this quote from Edith: "My search for the truth was a constant prayer."

5. How did Edith remain true to the faith and kind to her family in the face of her family's reaction to her becoming a Catholic and later a Carmelite?

6. How was Edith's life and death an act of atonement?

Quotes

Complete one or both of the following.

1. Choose one or more quotes from St. Edith Stein, memorize it/them, and recite it/them.

2. Choose a quote from St. Edith Stein and explain it in essay form. You may wish to give your composition as a speech.

Geography and History

Complete one or more of the following.

1. Using many of the place names in this biography, draw and label a map of the life and travels of St. Edith Stein in Germany and Holland. Note: there is little information about the exact route of her last train trip; some place names may have changed since the war.

2. Research and draw a map illustrating one or more aspects of Nazi occupation of other countries of Europe during World War II.

3. Research and write a brief report of the events in Germany leading up to World War II. You may start with the Franco-Prussian War of 1870, World War I in 1914, or the Nazi rise to power in 1932.

4. Research and write a brief historical biography on one or more of the following persons.

    a. Edmund Husserl

    b. Pope Pius XI

    c. Pope Pius XII

5. Adolf Reinach died during World War I at Flanders. Write a brief report of the significance of Flanders and its casualties during World War I. You may wish to include the famous poem by Carl Sandburg "In Flanders Field."

6. Edith nursed soldiers who had typhus, cholera, and dysentery. Write a brief report on these three diseases, describing each one's causes, onset, course, and treatment.

Research and Report

Choose one or more of the following topics, and research and write a report about it. Be sure to include related maps, diagrams, time lines, and illustrations.

1. World War II. (Especially the European Theater)

2. Discalced Carmelite Nuns (also known as the Teresian Carmel)

3. The Holocaust

4. The Resistance during World War II (include information on the Assisi Underground)

5. The Liturgical Year of the Catholic Church

You, The Biographer

Research and write a biography of one or more persons listed below. Be sure to use at least two sources for your biography. You may wish to present it as a speech.

1. St. Teresa of Avila, also known as St. Teresa of Jesus.

2. St. John of the Cross.

3. Esther, from the Old Testament.

Putting Your Faith into Practice

Choose one or more of the following.

1. Write an essay or speech telling how the life of St. Edith Stein is an inspiration for you to live a deeper Christian life.

2. Many Christians worldwide are imprisoned for their faith, and many are forced into slavery. Assist by your prayers, your funds, and perhaps your letter writing an organization that helps these people.

3. Next time you are at Mass, try to concentrate on every word and gesture the way St. Edith Stein did. In so doing, you will be giving good example.

4. Edith never forgot the good example of the woman with the shopping basket in Frankfort's cathedral. This woman did not know that she was a good influence on someone who would join the Church and become a saint. Perhaps you have been an inspiring example to someone. Write an essay describing the importance of giving good example. Who has inspired you?

5. Edith's broken wrist and ankle enabled her to see what she cherished most: Rosa's baptism. Write a story telling of an event in you own life where a greater good came out of disaster.

6. Edith Stein loved the liturgical year of the Church. Obtain a Catholic calendar or a guide to the liturgical year of the Church, and follow it each day for a period of three months. Determine the night before which saint or season is commemorated the next day, and prepare a prayer or reading accordingly. Read and/or pray in the morning, and think about the liturgical day during the day. You may wish to attend Mass, or obtain a Christian Prayer book that has the daily office of the Church, and pray Morning and Evening Prayer for the day. After the three months, reflect on how this has changed your life, your personality, and your outlook.

For more information contact:

Institute of Carmelite Studies
2131 Lincoln Road, NE
Washington, DC 20002-1199
www.icspublications.org

Blessed Francis Xavier Seelos

With Grateful Joy

Detroit, Michigan

September 1866

It was a gathering that everyone would remember. A large, festive crowd assembled one evening at St. Mary's parish to honor a priest who was leaving for another assignment the next morning. The city band arrived to play music, followed by the Light Guard Band at 8 p.m. This band, comprised of young people, played their best music as well, and the bandleader gave a speech honoring the priest. At 11 p.m. the St. Mary Choir led a huge crowd of men and women in singing songs to serenade their guest of honor.

Who was this priest who inspired such affection among the parishioners? One would think that it must have been a priest who served the parish for many years in order to be honored in such a way. But Fr. Francis Seelos had served at St. Mary for only ten months. Much of this time he had spent away from the parish giving retreats for priests and parish missions for lay people in other nearby cities. Despite this, he had made a huge impression on the parishioners of St. Mary's parish. Word got around, as it did in every city in which Fr. Seelos had worked as a priest, that he was a "holy priest."

Many people experienced his kindness in the confessional and in his sermons at Mass, and his love for the poor and distressed was legendary.

Fr. Van Emstede, his superior, was amazed at the lively display of affection for Fr. Seelos. He knew that Fr. Seelos made a habit of visiting the sick in their homes; Fr. Seelos had handed him a list of all the people whom he visited so that another priest could continue visiting them after his absence.

After opening and reading the list, Fr. Van Emstede was no longer amazed at his parishioners' gratitude toward Fr. Seelos. The sick list was very long, and made up of the very poorest, sick people. When these people later told him of how much Fr. Seelos had loved and consoled them, he knew why they held him in such esteem. Even the Bishop noticed the holiness of Fr. Seelos.

"I am sorry that Fr. Seelos must leave my diocese, for one had only to look at him to know he is a saint," said Bishop Lefevre.

After stopping in Chicago for a ten-day retreat, advisable before beginning a major assignment, Fr. Seelos traveled south by train, headed for New Orleans. Traveling with him was Brother Lawrence, a fellow member of the Redemptorist Order, founded by the great teacher, St. Alphonsus Liguori. On Father's mind and in his prayers were the tragic circumstances of his new assignment.

Four priests and three students from the Redemptorist seminary at Annapolis had gone for a boat ride in the Chesapeake Bay. After some time, one of the seminarians decided to go for a swim. In pain from cramps, he cried for help. One priest swam out to help him, and the men in the boat watched in horror as he disappeared under the waves. They tried to save both men, and did save the seminarian, but the priest was lost.

Their spirits heavy with sadness, they turned the boat toward shore and headed in. A sudden squall blew in and the boat overturned. They clung to the boat in the storm for as long as they could. Knowing that death was near, they had prayed aloud for God to have mercy on them. But as the strength of each one gave out, they slipped into the water one by one until only one priest and one seminarian were left alive in the morning when help came.

It was a terrible tragedy. The Redemptorists had come to the mission field of America from Germany and France, and already had attracted many Americans to the order to become priests.

Such a loss of three seminary instructors and two future priests was indeed a hard one for the Redemptorists to overcome. But overcome they did. A priest stationed in New Orleans was recalled to Annapolis to fill one of the teaching vacancies, and Fr. Seelos was transferred to New Orleans to take his place.

As he rode the train south, he remained in his seat all night. He could have taken a Pullman berth and slept, but he chose to be frugal with the order's money and with his time. Two School Sisters of Notre Dame also traveled on the same train. One of them, Sr. Maria Largusa, took notice of Fr. Seelos because of his special kindness and courtesy to the sisters. As he sat up all night, Fr. Seelos seemed to her to be praying constantly.

As she conversed with him in the morning, Sr. Maria asked him a question.

"Will you be in New Orleans long, Father?" she asked.

"I'll be there a year. Then I'll die of yellow fever," he said, smiling.

Amazed, Sr. Maria made sure that she remembered this remark. She was to learn much later that Fr. Seelos had said the same thing to a fellow Redemptorist a few months earlier. Sr. Maria wondered if Fr. Seelos had a special insight of some kind.

Fr. Seelos arrived at the Redemptorist parish in New Orleans. The people of New Orleans were a lively mixture of many languages, races, and nations, such as Germans, French Negroes, Creoles, and English. To serve all these people, the parish served by the Redemptorist priests was rather large. This parish consisted of three churches: St. Mary's of the Assumption for German-speaking people, St. Alphonsus for English-speaking people and Notre Dame de Bon Secours for the French-speaking. It was not unusual for the Redemptorists to help out at one another's parish churches.

It was like being right at home for Fr. Seelos when he arrived. Fr. Duffy, the superior of the Redemptorists, had been a student of Fr. Seelos when he taught at the Redemptorist seminary in Maryland many years ago.

"Now you can have your revenge on me for all the evil I did to you many years ago," joked Fr. Seelos.

Remembering the legendary kindness and wisdom shown to him by Fr. Seelos in those days, Fr. Duffy only smiled. Also present was Fr. Alexander Czvitkovicz, whose eloquent plea for Redemptorist missionary priests had brought Fr. Seelos to America in the first place. In his sixteen years as a Redemptorist, Fr. Seelos had served with, or been superior to, nearly all of the thirteen Redemptorists in New Orleans. He had come to a house full of old and dear friends.

Fr. Seelos was assigned to be the pastor of St. Mary's. He got down to work right away. He said Mass in such a way that each word and gesture was done in a reverent, loving way; those present at his Mass learned the importance of each part of the Mass by observing his recollected conduct. His face always smiling, Fr. Seelos preached sermons that emphasized the kindness of God and the confidence we should have in His Mercy. He performed marriages, visited the sick, and baptized infants. He taught catechism to the children of the school three times a week. Like his sermons at Mass, Fr. Seelos' catechism lessons were easy for the children to understand. He not only explained the Faith clearly to the children, but he had a way of making the Faith attractive to follow.

"His explanations were so simple that all the children could understand them, and at the same time they penetrated the heart," said one teacher.

His greatest successes were in the confessional. "If you are afraid of making your confession, come to me; I promise to be gentle with you," he would say from the pulpit at Mass.

He was so kind, and spoke so eloquently of the mercy of God, that hardened sinners reformed their lives after going to confession to him. Penitents who went to confession to him kept coming back because his advice was so good and beneficial for their souls. People of all backgrounds, the rich and the poor, the educated and the simple, traveled for miles and stood for hours in line just to make a general confession to Fr. Seelos.

"Whatever affliction you might have, if you went to Fr. Seelos, your affliction ceased before you came away," remembered Maria Hippler, a parishioner. The people of New Orleans quickly grew fond of him and were grateful for his consolation and guidance.

Fr. Seelos returned the affection of his parishioners. He had served at all the houses, or places the Redemptorists were stationed, in the Redemptorist province, or geographic area of service, in America, such as Baltimore, Pittsburgh, Annapolis, Cumberland, Detroit, and now New Orleans. He had also preached missions in Illinois, Connecticut, New York, Mississippi, West Virginia, and Rhode Island.

"I have made the rounds of all the houses in the province. Only New Orleans yet remains. I have come here to pass the rest of my days and find a lasting resting place at Saint Mary's. I feel I have traveled enough. I shall never leave New Orleans," he was fond of saying to his Redemptorist brothers.

Fr. Seelos received word that his mother died in the Seelos family hometown of Fussen in Germany, at the age of seventy-eight. He was grateful for the time she had spent teaching him to practice and to love the Catholic Faith. Fr. Seelos had remarked to his seminary students that if he ever saw his mother again, he would fall on his knees and kiss her feet for all that she had done for him. He admired her very much, and offered many Masses for the repose of her soul.

"Dear Mother," he had written years before, "how I thank you for having taught us children a great devotion to the Mother of God. Such an inheritance from parents is worth more than gold or silver." The devotion that Fr. Seelos had to the Mother of God was the channel for his holiness and for all the good he was able to do for souls. Looking back on his childhood, Fr. Seelos was grateful to God for having given him such devout parents.

As a former instructor and rector of the Redemptorist seminary, Fr. Seelos was zealous to encourage young men to the religious life. Many men had Fr. Seelos to thank for encouraging their vocations to the priesthood and the religious life. One young man of New Orleans, eighteen-year-old Joseph Schwartz, wanted to become a religious, but did not receive much encouragement. Schwartz' schooling was interrupted by the Civil War, and he needed more education in order to be ready and prepared for further seminary studies. This was the main problem.

Fr. Seelos met the young man, and upon learning that he wished to be a religious, questioned him at length. After listening attentively to the young man, he told Schwartz that he would make a fine Redemptorist, and encouraged him to apply for admission. Joseph Schwartz was accepted, and became a good priest with a distinguished career of service.

In future years he would serve at the Redemptorist seminaries in America, and was to become the procurator general in Rome, where he also taught seminarians among whom he became something of a legend. He was forever grateful for the encouragement Fr. Seelos had given him.

The same thing happened in New Orleans as had happened in each place in which Fr. Seelos had lived. He acquired a reputation for working miracles by his prayers. He did nothing to encourage this reputation, and much to discourage it, but this reputation grew because facts backed it up. A man named George Segal had a three-year-old daughter who was deathly ill. She had a high fever, was refusing to eat, and was growing more and more frail. The desperate father and mother brought her to Fr. Seelos, who prayed over her. She got worse as they watched. Fr. Seelos advised the family to go home and have all their workers pray together for the child. This was done immediately. The child got better that night. The Segals brought the little girl to Fr. Seelos two more times for prayers, and she improved each time. The child recovered completely, and enjoyed good health after her ordeal.

Maria Jost, the widow who washed clothes for the Redemptorists, was injured by a terrible accident. She was crossing the street at an intersection, balancing a basketful of the Redemptorist's wash on her head, when a horse-drawn trolley struck her. She was so injured that for two months she lay in bed, unable to move at all without help. For a woman used to working all her life, this must have been intolerable. The doctors told her that after another month in bed, she might be able to get up for very short periods.

Fr. Seelos visited her, and began to speak to her of the virtue of patience.

"I would rather die than stay helpless in bed for another month," she said firmly.

Fr. Seelos then prayed for her and blessed her. The next morning she got up and got down to work as if she never had been injured. She was firmly convinced of the power of Fr. Seelos' prayers for the rest of her life.

Fr. Neithart, who served with Fr. Seelos in New Orleans, summarizes his last year of life:

> The amount of daily labor he performed as chief pastor of Saint Mary's, prefect of the church, prefect of the brothers, spiritual director of the sisters and of thousands of seculars, was truly astonishing.

> None of us ever saw him idle for a moment. He never went visiting, never sat talking in the parlor, but was always to be found either in his cell writing or praying, or else in the confessional, in the schools, or on sick calls. Indeed, he literally killed himself with labor, mortifications, and exertions. Nevertheless, he was the most cheerful and humorous of the community.

In early August of 1867 was the first outbreak of an unusually strong epidemic of yellow fever. By the middle of September the death toll had climbed to sixty-seven people a day! All of New Orleans was affected; mosquitoes spread yellow fever, and the method for controlling the outbreak of the disease had not been perfected yet.

The only thing to do once a person came down with it was to keep them comfortable and hope for recovery. Many did not make it.

Even the Redemptorists caught yellow fever. Since so many people were sick with this sometimes fatal disease, they sent word to the Fathers to visit them and give them the Sacrament of Extreme Unction. All the requested sick calls were written on a slate in the Fathers' parlor. Each priest took as many sick calls as he could, and erased them from the list. In this way, he hoped to save work for his brother priests.

At first, the priests made the sick calls on foot, but a kind man called Mr. McKendrick arranged for a horse and buggy to be sent to the rectory for the priests to use; they were able to make more sick calls this way. This relieved the priests, especially Fr. Seelos, for their main worry was that they would not be able to visit each sick person before death. To die with the Sacraments is the greatest consolation for a Catholic.

The priests worked at a brisk pace, so brisk that one by one they got sick with yellow fever. Two fathers were down. This made more work for the others. Fr. Seelos redoubled his efforts, and visited as many sick as he could. He visited one little girl who had yellow fever.

"I will offer my own life for her," Fr. Seelos told the girl's astonished mother.

"But Father, such an act is too much to expect!" the woman replied.

On September 17, Fr. Seelos was not his usual cheerful self at lunchtime. He appeared depressed and tired, but asked Fr. Duffy's permission to make a promised sick call.

Concerned for him, and believing that a walk outdoors might make him feel better, Fr. Duffy agreed. When Fr. Seelos returned at three o'clock, he was so ill that he was put to bed. Although his fever was high, the doctor believed that Fr. Seelos had a mild case of yellow fever because he was so cheerful and uncomplaining.

Before long, four priests and two brothers were in bed with yellow fever. Fr. Seelos asked many times a day about the condition of his stricken brothers, and he prayed for them. The first to die was Brother Lawrence, who had been Fr. Seelos' traveling companion on his train trip to New Orleans. He had served the Redemptorists as a carpenter, mechanic, and architect, and had been a strong man who seemed nearly indestructible.

Brother Gerard was in a bad way, too. One of the brothers watched by his bedside. "I would like to die, but I cannot," said Brother Gerard to him. He died the next day, accepting the will of God. The grieving Redemptorists buried the brothers together, and cared for their sick. Three of the priests were recovering slowly, but Fr. Seelos remained weak.

By October 1, Fr. Seelos' pulse became rapid and his breathing shallow, and he was rapidly weakening. The doctor was amazed that Fr. Seelos had hung on so long, and told Fr. Duffy that the end was near. Fr. Duffy, heartbroken, volunteered to tell the patient the news.

"Father Seelos, the doctor says you are going to heaven," said Fr. Duffy, his voice unsteady with grief.

"So the doctor says I am to die! Oh, what pleasant news! How thankful I am! And to you, doctor, how much I have to return thanks for your kindness and attention to me!" replied Fr. Seelos from his sickbed.

*   *   *

Who was this man who so cheerfully accepted death?

Francis Xavier Seelos was born on January 11, 1819, in the town of Fussen, in Bavaria. He was baptized the same day. He was the sixth of twelve children born to Magnus and Frances Seelos. Xavier, as the family called him, was very sickly, so much so that he was not expected to survive childhood. He had serious stomach ailments that confined him to bed for long periods of time. As a result, he spent a lot of time with his mother as she went about her household duties.

Concerned that he would die young, Frau Seelos constantly taught the Catholic Faith to her son. She had a strong, vibrant faith, and taught Xavier a devotion to prayer, especially the Rosary, and a love of virtue. Of all her children, Xavier seemed to learn these lessons the best.

Some of the favorite times the Seelos children had were when Frau Seelos read the stories of the saints to them. On one occasion, she read the story of the famous missionary of the Far East, St. Francis Xavier. Inspired by the story of masculine courage, fortitude, and devotion, young Xavier exclaimed, "I will be a Francis Xavier!" Frau Seelos remembered this remark, as did her daughter, Antonia, and in this remark they both saw the seeds of a future priestly vocation for Xavier.

Magnus Seelos, usually called Mang, was a devoted father. He was an unfailingly cheerful and genial man who worked as a clothmaker to support his family. He, like his wife, had a strong Catholic faith. His own birth was something of a miracle. His mother had already lost two children when she became pregnant with him. She worried that she would lose this baby, too. When she learned that Pope Pius VI would be staying briefly in Fussen, she was determined to receive his papal blessing in the hope that it would secure for her a safe and happy delivery of her child.

She went to the place where the Pope stood outside to bless the people, and as he did so, Frau Seelos prayed that her baby would live and be healthy. Her prayer was heard. She gave birth to Magnus Seelos, who enjoyed robust health and a robust faith all his life. Sadly, Frau Seelos died two years later. His father remarried a good woman who was a devoted mother to him.

Mang spent some years traveling in France as a young man while learning the trade of clothmaker. This enabled him to esteem the good qualities of people of other languages and countries. He passed on this esteem to his children; for Xavier it was to bear fruit in his missionary work with all kinds of people.

One of Xavier's sisters remembered how their home life influenced the Seelos children:

> In our home the daily routine was as follows. The whole family arose early and went to Mass. After breakfast each one went to his accustomed work and the children went to school. Before meals the Angelus was recited and prayers were said at table.

> During the meal the children had to relate what they had learned in school, to which Father added a few comments. After dinner we all returned to our occupations. No one was allowed to be idle even for a quarter of an hour. When supper was finished, we had spiritual reading, which was always on the life of the saint of the day.

All of the Seelos children grew up to be exemplary Catholics. Nine children grew to adulthood. Elizabeth, Ambrose, and Adam married; Josephine, Antonia, and Kunigunda remained single; and Frances, Anna, and Xavier entered religious life.

Mang brought home an abandoned baby boy one day, and laid him on the kitchen table in front of his surprised wife, saying, "There, we have another child. One more will not make much difference." Lovingly they raised John as their own son.

Xavier attended Catholic school in town. He received the Sacrament of Confirmation in 1828, and made his First Holy Communion in 1830. The large family was poor, and money was scarce. Mang was a good clothmaker, but the factories of the Industrial Revolution were able to make cloth cheaper and more plentiful. That same year, an opportunity presented itself to Mang, and he took it. He became the sacristan of St. Magnus Church. He held the keys to the church, and took care of all of its upkeep, from building maintenance to getting the holy vessels ready for morning Mass. The income was small but steady, and a house was provided for the sacristan and his family.

The Seelos family loved their larger house with its garden, but most of all, they loved being so close to church. Xavier loved to help his father at his job, and he served as many Masses as he could. He accompanied his mother to church to say the Rosary.

Xavier neared the end of his schooling; after six years, he could either learn a trade or go on for more schooling. He was too frail to qualify for a trade, and he was an excellent student. The only thing standing in the way of further schooling was money. The Seelos family still was poor. Xavier had learned to "do without" cheerfully and without complaining, but this problem was beyond him.

Frau Seelos' brother was a priest, and he offered to help Xavier with tuition. The family was happy that Xavier would get the education he needed, and grateful for their uncle's generosity. But unfortunately, Xavier's uncle died suddenly. Now what should he do?

The new pastor of St. Magnus took an interest in Xavier, and spoke to him about his future. "Francis, you ought to go on for higher studies, since you are too weak for manual labor," said Fr. Heim.

"If my uncle had not died, things would be different," replied Xavier sadly. But Fr. Heim was determined to help the tall boy. Another day, he again urged Xavier to pursue his education. Mang happened to be nearby and overheard the remark.

"My dear pastor, as much as I would like to see my Xavier study, my circumstances will not permit it," said Mang.

"No! No! as you will soon see. I was in Augsburg; I have good friends there. If you can help a little, I think an arrangement can be made to send Xavier to Augsburg this coming autumn," said the zealous young priest. Xavier felt as though his spirit suddenly had wings.

Fr. Heim helped Xavier apply for admission to St. Stephen's in Augsburg, and to apply for the necessary scholarships. It was a long wait, but by the autumn of 1832, Xavier's dream had come true. He was a student at St. Stephen's.

Xavier was a good student. He liked the religious atmosphere of the school, where in addition to their regular classes students attended Mass daily and studied theology and philosophy. He boarded with one family, but his daily meals were not included in the arrangement. Xavier had lunch alternately with two different families, and shifted for himself for breakfast and dinner; usually these meals consisted only of dry bread. Xavier did what he could to earn extra money, such as cleaning the rooms of other students. He remained cheerful no matter what his circumstances. Other students were poorer still than he. These had no regular meals at all. If he had any money in his pocket, he often gave it to these students, earning the nickname "The Banker." Someone remarked to Seelos that he did not have much himself.

"They are poorer than I. They have no house to get breakfast and they have no money. I cannot see them in need while I have anything," he said. When he went home for vacation, he often brought a poorer student with him to enjoy long walks in the mountains and his happy family atmosphere. This readiness to share what he had was evident in him all his life.

Years passed. Seelos did well in school, learning several languages. After six years he was graduated from St. Stephen's. He was accepted for another scholarship, and he attended the school of philosophy in the Royal Ludwig Maximilian University at Munich in the fall of 1839. His favorite courses were in theology. During his three years in Munich, he decided to become a priest.

Seelos tutored other students to earn extra money. He also gave his brother, Adam, lessons in reading and writing. One day Seelos told his brother, "We will have no writing today. The Blessed Virgin has appeared to me tonight and told me to become a missionary." He was already interested in the Redemptorist Order when a plea came from America for more Redemptorist missionary priests to serve abandoned Germans there. Fr. Alexander Czvitkovicz wrote an eloquent plea in the local paper, offering interested young men the chance to finish their studies for the priesthood in the Redemptorist seminary in America. Seelos applied early in 1842, and he waited.

He went home for his usual vacation, and he seemed to his family to be somewhat sad. He confided only in Mang, who approved of his plans, even though he was sad to see his son go so far away. Seelos tried to soak up all the sights and sounds of home to remember in the future. He especially regretted leaving his sister, Antonia, who was his closest friend. When the family said goodbye to him, Mang pointed skyward. The family was puzzled at this, but Seelos knew that his father meant that they would be reunited in heaven.

The Redemptorists accepted Seelos in November of 1842. As he made preparations to sail to America, Seelos resolved not to return home. He loved his family so much that he feared that seeing them again would make him change his mind. For him, the will of God was clear, and he strove to carry it out, no matter what it cost him. He wrote each family member long letters. To Antonia he wrote: "I am writing this letter in tears … but my heart is filled with complete abandonment to the Holy Will of God. I sing the praises of Divine Providence. I make my sacrifice willingly, although with a very heavy heart …"

Seelos sailed from Le Havre, France, on a ship called the St. Nicholas on March 18, 1843, and arrived in New York City a month later. He traveled to Baltimore, Maryland, where the Redemptorists had their novitiate. Seelos became a novice in the Redemptorist Order. He spent the next year and a half studying the rule, or way of life, of his order. Seelos loved his time in the novitiate, and used his time there to grow closer to God.

He wrote to his family: "In peace and quiet I was able to make my novitiate while learning the duties of a cleric. I learned to love the spiritual life and its treasures more and more. God planted deep in my heart the desire to offer myself completely to Him. This desire grows from day to day, so that I want to give God more than I have ever done before, all ever held dear, all to which my heart was once attached."

Francis Xavier Seelos was ordained a priest on December 22, 1844, and said his first Mass on Christmas Day. He remembered his family in a special way that day, for his dream had become their dream, too. He wrote them letters full of priestly advice and familial affection, and was a devoted letter-writer all his life. While waiting for his assignment, Fr. Seelos helped out at St. James in Baltimore. It was a parish of many languages and races. Fr. Seelos was still mastering the English language as he preached his first sermons. Nevertheless, he impressed his congregation. One Irish lady said, "It does me good to see that holy priest struggle so hard."

Finally, Fr. Seelos received his priestly assignment; he was to go to St. Philomena Parish in Pittsburgh, Pennsylvania. He was to serve there for nine years. Twenty-one Redemptorist priests served forty-five thousand Catholics over a large geographic area. The area's many factories made the air so sooty that the hands of schoolchildren soiled the paper on which they wrote before they finished their assignments.

There was a great deal of anti-Catholic sentiment in Pittsburgh, as there was in most of America. This was propagated by the Know-Nothings, an anti-Catholic group of men who responded to any question about their group with the same answer: "We know nothing." They slandered priests and Catholics, and published their lies in books and newspapers. The Redemptorists knew that they had to counter the lies of these men so that young Catholics would not be tempted to give up the faith for fear of persecution by these intimidators. They did this by preaching the truth of the Catholic Faith, and providing the sacraments so that Catholics would be strong in God's grace.

The Redemptorists had a lot to contend with from the Know-Nothings. They set fire to St. Philomena School, and only the quick thinking of a Catholic wagon driver who happened to drive past in the middle of the night saved the school from destruction. One priest taking the Blessed Sacrament to a sick person rode in a stagecoach. His fellow passengers began to use bad language, and he kindly asked them to stop. Their impure language turned abusive, and the driver, who advised the priest to get out and walk, stopped them from killing the priest. On another occasion, the Know-Nothings publicly accused the Redemptorists of stockpiling guns and ammunition with which they intended to slay Protestants. An unruly mob, inflamed with these lies, almost did the Fathers harm. One of their leaders agreed to tour the Redemptorist buildings, and saw only the poor holdings of those who served the poor, sheltered orphans, taught children, and provided the sacraments. Surprised, he told the Know-Nothings that there were no guns at all.

Fr. Seelos' superior was Fr. John Neumann, now known as St. John Neumann. Fr. Neumann encouraged Fr. Seelos to dive right into parish life. Soon he was hearing confessions, baptizing, offering Mass, preaching, teaching catechism to children, and going on sick calls. Fr. Seelos watched Fr. Neumann carry out his priestly duties, and was impressed with his holiness. He strove to imitate him, and was grateful for his good example. Years later he wrote:

> In every respect [St. John Neumann] was a remarkable father to me. … He cared for all my needs in body and soul; above all, the example of his virtues is vivid in my memory, his tender modesty, his great humility and his insuperable patience. Our dwelling was so poor that one night we had to leave our room in a severe storm and seek protection elsewhere, because the water was pouring down on our beds. I say our room because we were in one and the same room, which was separated only by a curtain. For that reason I could hear him often saying his prayers during the night. He slept so little that I could not understand how he could keep his body and soul together. Because he generally got up before the regular rising time, he prepared the fire, often bringing up coal himself to have the room warm for me when I got up.

The Redemptorist Fathers served many towns in outlying areas. They went wherever there were Catholics who wanted Holy Mass. Fr. Seelos often offered Mass outdoors in Sharpsburg where St. Mary's Church was being built. One Sunday, it began to rain. Fr. Seelos was soaked, and many of the people scattered for shelter.

Fr. Seelos asked them to stay, in the rain, to make reparation for the sins they had committed. They stayed until Mass was over. From then on, it never rained during an outdoor Mass until the church building was finished!

People crowded to hear Fr. Seelos' sermons. His preaching was easy to understand, yet it inspired zeal for the faith, and "went right to the heart" of his parishioners. Fifty years later they still acclaimed his sermons. The faithfulness with which Fr. Seelos carried out his priestly duties was what impressed his parishioners the most. He put the faith into practice.

He took time to teach schoolchildren their catechism, and was very patient with them. He was never angry, but always was gentle and patient with the children and their questions. None dared be rude to such an exemplary priest. Many were the young men whom he helped to find their religious vocations. Such was the esteem in which the parishioners of St. Philomena held him that when Fr. Seelos had a bout of illness, adults and schoolchildren alike made special visits to the Blessed Sacrament to pray for his recovery!

Fr. Seelos prayed for mercy, and also practiced it. An old schoolmate, fallen on hard times, was dressed in shabby clothes. Upon meeting him again, Fr. Seelos gave the man his own shoes. He gave a poor woman his own gloves. Another woman with small children was on her deathbed. "I am not afraid to die, but I am worried about my little children," she told

Fr. Seelos.

"Then pray a novena in honor of the Blessed Sacrament and receive Holy Communion. Ask God to restore your health with the same confidence shown by the woman who touched the hem of Christ's garment," advised Fr. Seelos. The woman did so, and she recovered completely!

Parents of sick children brought them to Fr. Seelos in church, and he prayed over them before the altar of Our Lady with such confidence that the children were cured. A girl had epilepsy, and had never been to school. Fr. Seelos prayed over her, and told her mother to send the girl to school. The fearful mother kept her home, and the girl had another seizure. The mother brought the girl back to Fr. Seelos, who prayed over her at the special altar dedicated to Our Lady. He told the woman to send the girl to school, and finally she did so. The epilepsy vanished, and the girl enjoyed good health.

A man on crutches struggled painfully to the rectory to see Fr. Seelos, and asked him to bless and cure him. "I do not have power to cure you," began Fr. Seelos. The man then threw his crutches out the rectory window. "I'm not leaving until you cure me," he said. Fr. Seelos gave the man his priestly blessing, amazed at his strong faith in the blessing of a priest. Instantly cured, the man walked home.

His sister, Kunnigunda, died in a tragic accident in 1851. She was storing hay in the attic of the family home when she fell three stories to the pavement. Praying "Lord, I am not worthy!" she lingered only three hours until she died. Mang prayed, "God gave her to me and God has taken her from me. Blessed be the Name of the Lord!" Her sister, Elizabeth, who saw it happen, became paralyzed on one side and was bedridden for the rest of her life. Mang had a stroke shortly thereafter, and died two years later. Fr. Seelos consoled his family by letter and prayer, and he remembered his father's parting gesture as he left home. He was grateful for such a good father.

In 1854, Fr. Seelos was transferred to St. Alphonsus Parish in Baltimore. It was a busy, lively place. Its school had fifteen hundred children, and there were many orders of sisters who served the poor, the sick, and orphaned children in the parish. He wrote to his sister:

> I cannot thank God enough for my vocation, although from morning till night I am overwhelmed with cares and worries. ... White and Negro, German and English, confreres and externs, clerical and lay people, aristocratic women and unworldly nuns, the poor, the sick, ask for my assistance. One wants this, the other that. There is no rest. ... But often in the midst of all this work I do something dumb and everything goes topsy-turvy. Nothing astonishes me more than the extent of the patience which the dear Lord displays in my regard. ... My greatest consolation is that so many and such good people pray for me, among whom you, my dear Sister, are surely not the least.

In 1857, Fr. Seelos received a new assignment and became the prefect of students at the Redemptorist Seminary; he also taught dogmatic theology and sacred Scripture. Fr. Seelos was "in his element." He considered the formation of future priests to be very important work, and he was a true father to his seminarians, even cleaning their muddy shoes himself.

It was customary in those days to be strict, even harsh with students. Fr. Seelos did not behave this way. Rather, he instructed his students with gentleness and understanding. His amiable requests got more cooperation than the gruff orders of his brother priests.

The students liked him very much, and seemed to know that he was a saintly priest. They watched his conduct and listened to his words, and tried to learn as much as they could from him so they could better imitate his holiness. For example, they noticed that he did not season his food, and ate whatever was put before him. He seemed to always have his Rosary in hand, and said it constantly in such a way that it was hardly noticeable, especially when he was walking someplace. Often they found him sleeping on the floor, his bed untouched. When he was unfairly criticized, he bore it patiently. "Prayer must be my chief strength," he said. The seminarians that knew him remembered his good example all their lives.

Not all of his brother priests approved of his gentle methods. One of them thought he was "too weak", and started a letter-writing campaign to have Fr. Seelos removed from his assignment in 1860. This was the same year in which Fr. Seelos was one of the priests nominated to succeed Bishop O'Connor. He pleaded for his name to be dropped from consideration, and it was. Sadly, this letter-writing campaign was successful, and in 1863 Fr. Seelos began work in the home missions. He said not one word of complaint about his removal from office.

Perhaps he looked upon his new post as a blessing in disguise. As much as Fr. Seelos liked teaching future priests, he liked the missions more. "I love the work of the missions more than all other labors; it is a complete apostolic employment in the Lord's vineyard," he wrote. A parish mission is a series of sermons preached in a parish by a visiting priest or priests to intensify the spiritual life of the faithful, and to bring lapsed Catholics back to the Church. Along with their inspiring sermons, the priests offered many opportunities for confession as well. Travel was often grueling. It was the middle of the Civil War, and the Redemptorists often had to travel on slow trains with lots of soldiers. Along with his fellow missioners, Fr. Seelos traveled through Missouri, Illinois, Michigan, Ohio, Pennsylvania, New Jersey, New York, and Rhode Island. Lodging was often primitive, and sometimes was at a distance from the parish in which they preached. Nonetheless, Fr. Seelos was an enthusiastic home missioner. The people to whom he preached were often appallingly ignorant of their Catholic Faith because they had no priest to explain it to them. Saving souls was his first priority. He carefully wrote out the texts for many different kinds of sermons so that he could reach as many souls as possible.

Word got out, as it did wherever Fr. Seelos went, that he was a "holy priest," and people traveled twenty and even thirty miles by horse and wagon to hear him preach and to go to confession to him. He had amazing success converting hardened sinners. "God blesses the missions in a wonderful way. Many poor and abandoned souls are reunited with Him," he wrote.

What was his secret for success? First, of course, it was his reliance on prayer, but second, it was his faith in the mercy of God. Sinners who lived sinful lives, and those negligent in the practice of their faith often thought that they themselves were "past saving." Not Fr. Seelos. To a mission audience he said:

> Oh, if only all the sinners of the whole wide world were present here! Yes, even the greatest, the most hardened, even those close to despair, I would call out to them. 'The Lord God is merciful and gracious, patient and of much compassion.' (Exodus 34:6) I would show them why the Apostles call God the Father of Mercy, the God of all consolation. I would tell them that the prophet in the Old Testament even said that the earth is full of the mercy of God and that mercy is above all His works. Oh, how can I make this clear to you? First, that God is filled with pity and invites us lovingly to come to Him; secondly, that God waits for the conversion of the whole world with patience; and thirdly, that God received the repentant sinner with Love!

He then appealed to Our Lady:

> O, Mother of Mercy! You understood the Mercy of God when you cried out in the Magnificat – 'His mercy is from generation to generation.' Obtain for all sinners a childlike confidence in the Mercy of God!

It was no wonder that people lined up at his confessional!

One day when they were traveling, his brother priests noticed that he had eaten nothing that day. They urged him to eat, but he said that he was doing penance for one of his penitents whose confession he had heard. One of the priests recalled that a notorious drunkard had gone to confession to Fr. Seelos, and concluded that he was fasting so that the man might persevere in virtue.

In 1866 Fr. Seelos went to Detroit. Although he continued to give missions, he also helped out at St. Mary's parish, and the parishioners quickly grew to love him.

As Fr. Seelos lay dying in his bed, Brother Louis knew the end was near, so he stayed by Father's deathbed and took care of him. Fr. Seelos lapsed in and out of consciousness; occasionally he would begin the prayers for Mass, unaware of where he was. At other times, his mind was clear. "Have you seen Our Blessed Mother?" asked Brother Louis, aware that she often visits the deathbeds of those who especially love her. "Oh, yes!" whispered Fr. Seelos.

Brother Louis' knee was aching, with all the running up and down stairs he did to take care of the sick Redemptorists. He asked Fr. Seelos to cure it for him. "What peculiar ideas you have!" said the good-natured priest. Brother Louis put his knee up on the bed beside the sick man. Fr. Seelos touched it, and immediately the pain ceased, and gave Brother no trouble for the rest of the yellow fever epidemic.

Fr. Duffy too had a knee problem. As a child, he had split his kneecap with an ax, and had almost lost the leg; the fervent prayers of his mother had saved it from amputation. With so many priests down with yellow fever, Fr. Duffy was making sick calls at a punishing pace, and his knee threatened to give out permanently. He went to Fr. Seelos' bedside. Finding him asleep, Fr. Duffy knelt on his one good knee and prayed to God that his bad knee would be cured through the merits and holiness of the dying priest. He felt a strange sensation. When he stood up, his knee was completely well, and he had no trouble with it for the rest of his life.

The Redemptorists gathered at his bedside. "I never thought it was so sweet to die in the Congregation. I now begin to know what happiness it is to live and die a Redemptorist. Oh, let us love our vocation and strive to persevere in it! Then everything will be all right with us!" said Fr. Seelos. The priests and brothers sang one of his favorite Marian hymns, one composed by St. Stanislaus Koska. With his eyes on the crucifix, Fr. Seelos died. It was October 4, 1867. He was forty-six years old.

New Orleans was in the midst of a hurricane, but that did not keep people away from the church in which Fr. Seelos' body lay. Christine Holle was very sick with terrible pains in her abdomen and hip.

She struggled to St. Mary's Church, and touched the hand of Fr. Seelos. She was instantly cured. The church was filled to capacity for the funeral Mass. Cries filled St. Mary's as Fr. Seelos was buried the next day in church near the statue of the Sorrowful Mother.

The faithful were not deprived of Fr. Seelos' help by his death. A little girl who was ill with smallpox was cured after her relatives asked for Fr. Seelos' prayers. A little boy, dying from measles, meningitis, and pneumonia recovered completely the moment his grandmother offered the Blessed Sacrament at the Mass she attended in honor of Fr. Seelos, whom she asked in prayer to cure her grandson.

Even recently, Fr. Seelos visited sick children in the hospital and blessed them, after which they were mysteriously cured of their ailments. Later seeing a holy card with the portrait of Fr. Seelos, to whom their relatives have been praying, the children excitedly identified him as the priest who had blessed them. Told that he died over one hundred years ago, the children insisted that it was he who had visited them!

Fr. Seelos continued to help people years and years after his death, and many different people had stories to tell of his saving help.

Blessed Father Seelos, pray for us!

Lesson Activities
Bl. Francis Xavier Seelos

Vocabulary

Define the following:

comprise	recollected	vocation	prefect
parishioner	rector	genial	amiable
parish mission	reputation	esteem	apostolic
retreat	mortification	sacristan	grueling
seminarian	consolation	reparation	negligent

Terms to Know

Discover the meaning of each of the following.

Yellow fever

Redemptorist

Missionary

Divine Providence

Catechism

Comprehension Questions

Answer the following, using complete sentences.

1. A huge crowd of people gathered at St. Mary's parish in Detroit to say goodbye to Fr. Seelos. How long had he served there?

2. Give at least three reasons that Fr. Seelos was so well-liked.

3. On the train to New Orleans, Sr. Maria asked Fr. Seelos if he would be in New Orleans long. What did he answer her?

4. Why was it like "being right at home" for Fr. Seelos when he arrived at the Redemptorist parish in New Orleans?

5. Why did people travel so far and wait so long to go to confession to Fr. Seelos?

6. Why was Fr. Seelos so grateful to his mother?

7. What did Fr. Seelos reply to the news Fr. Duffy gave him that he was going to die?

8. As a child, Xavier was sickly, and so was confined to bed for long periods of time. Why was this a blessing in disguise?

9. Mang Seelos became the sacristan of St. Magnus Church. How did Xavier benefit from this?

10. How did Xavier earn the nickname "The Banker"?

11. Why did Seelos sail for America without saying goodbye in person to his family?

12. Fr. Seelos was stationed in Pittsburgh for many years. What about him impressed his parishioners the most?

13. Parents of sick children brought them to Fr. Seelos. What did he do?

14. Fr. Seelos' seminary students watched his conduct so they could better imitate his holiness. Tell at least three things that they noticed about him.

15. Fr. Seelos knew great mission success in his preaching and in the confessional. What was his secret for success?

Analyze This

Using as many details as you can, explain each question in paragraph form.

1. Why did the parishioners of St. Mary's Church in Detroit esteem Fr. Seelos so much?

2. How did Fr. Seelos serve the people of New Orleans?

3. In what ways was Fr. Seelos a healing priest?

4. How did yellow fever reduce the ranks of the Redemptorists?

5. What elements went into making the Seelos home life so exemplary?

6. What in his upbringing influenced Fr. Seelos to be a self-sacrificing person?

7. What injustices did Fr. Seelos suffer under, and how did he deal with each one?

8. What accounted for the many conversions for which Fr. Seelos was responsible?

Essay Questions

Answer one or more of the following in essay form.

1. Fr. Seelos had a special love and concern for the poor and the sick all his life. How could the events of his life have influenced this concern?

2. Fr. Seelos had a kindly, genial approach to people. How was this such an effective approach, and why?

3. In the life of Fr. Seelos, how have tragedies turned into blessings?

4. What people and events in the youth of Fr. Seelos influenced his conduct as an adult?

5. In what ways did the conduct of St. John Neumann influence the priestly life of Fr. Seelos?

6. What virtues did Fr. Seelos exemplify in his life?

Quotes

Complete one or both of the following.

1. Choose one or more quotations by Fr. Seelos, memorize it/them, and recite it/them.

2. Choose a quote by Fr. Seelos, and explain it or comment on it in essay form. You may wish to give your essay as a speech.

Geography and History

Complete one or more of the following.

1. Sketch and label a map with the places in America where Fr. Seelos worked and visited.

2. Sketch out a brief report on the American Civil War. Include information on how New Orleans was affected.

3. Research and draw a map of the places in Germany where young Fr. Seelos lived.

4. Research and report on ship travel across the Atlantic Ocean in the 1800's. You may wish to draw a sailing ship.

Research and Report

Choose one or more of the following topics, and research and write a report about it. Be sure to include related maps, diagrams, time lines, and illustrations.

1. The Redemptorist Order: Its Purpose, Mission, and Charism.

2. The Missionary Efforts of the Redemptorist Order in America.

3. City of New Orleans: Its History and People.

4. Missions in America.

5. Immigration in America in the 1800's.

6. The Sacrament of Extreme Unction, or Anointing of the Sick.

You, The Biographer

Research and write a biography of one or more persons listed below. Be sure to use at least two sources for your biography. You may wish to present it as a speech.

1. St. Francis Xavier

1. St. Alphonsus Liguori

3. St. John Neumann

Science and Life

1. What is yellow fever? Research and report on its symptoms, onset, course, and past and current treatment.

2. Research to discover the condition of medical care for a person living in the 1800's. How have today's medicines changed things for today's sick person?

Putting Your Faith into Practice

Choose one or more of the following.

1. Fr. Seelos was a missionary who influenced countless people by his example. How can you help the missions?

   a. Earn some money and donate it to a missionary organization.

   b. Pray for missionaries and the missions every day. You may wish to compose your own prayer.

c. Decide how you can be a missionary by your good example. Write up a plan to do so, and carry out your plan.

2. "Prayer will be my chief strength," said Fr. Seelos. How can more frequent prayer influence you for the better? Determine to rely on a brief prayer before any undertaking, and see what a difference it makes.

3. How do your parents influence you to be a good person? Write them a thank-you letter for all they do for you and for their good example.

For more information contact:

Seelos Center
2030 Constance Street
New Orleans, LA 70130
www.seelos.org

Answer Key to
Reading Comprehension Questions

Below are the complete answers to each comprehension question. Wording need not be exact, but as long as the answer conveys the proper meaning, it is correct. If a reader understands the question in a different way than intended by the author, and can prove his or her answer from the text, the answer is also considered correct.

St. Gianna Beretta Molla

1. It grew at a fast rate and was increasingly painful. *or* Its fast growth would crowd the baby or harm Gianna.

2. The doctors could remove the cyst, remove the womb, and end the life of the baby; Gianna would not be able to have more children. The doctors could remove the cyst and end the life of the baby; Gianna might be able to have more children. The doctors could remove the cyst and let the baby grow; Gianna's life was in danger with this choice.

3. Gianna regarded all life as sacred, and each child as a blessing from God. *or* Her vocation as a mother was a precious gift to her by God.

4. Both of her parents were lay Franciscans and Gianna herself put into practice the Franciscan ideal of holy joy, self-sacrifice, and love of neighbor all her life.

5. The family's only real luxury was a good Catholic education for the children.

6. The Beretta parents encouraged their children in school so that each would be able to follow a profession and serve others.

7. The Eucharist was the key to Gianna's character. *or* Because she received Jesus every day, Gianna could better exemplify the virtues of Jesus in her life.

8. The subject of this retreat was the Four Last Things: death, judgment, heaven, and hell.

9. She was active in Catholic Action, she served the poor, and she enjoyed beautiful things.

10. She struggled with joining her brother in the Mission field as a doctor or marrying and forming a family.

11. Her three tools were prayers to God for guidance, advice from wise persons, and her own mind.

12. ... so too does it need good Christian families.

13. She wrote Pietro letters full of affection and news of the children.

14. Gianna wanted the both of them to choose life together.

15. "Thank you, Mother. Thank you for having given me life twice: in conception and when you permitted me to be born, deciding for my life. Intercede so that all mothers and families may always come to you with confidence."

Bl. Junipero Serra

1. Reading the lives of the saints inspired him.

2. An insect, probably a spider, mosquito, or scorpion, bit his leg, which remained infected and painful.

3. He believed in celebrating the sacraments with as much splendor as possible.

4. Fr. Serra celebrated Mass with reverence and splendor. He put on dramas and pageants to reenact the life of Christ. He put on a Christmas pageant. He reenacted the events of the Last Supper on Holy Thursday. He erected a large crucifix for Good Friday. He led Rosary processions.

5. They must have been the Holy Family.

6. Galvez received orders to arrange an expedition to occupy Upper California for Spain.

7. First, Spain looked upon Upper California as its own territory. Second, Spain was worried that Russian settlements were moving south into their territory.

8. A poultice of herbs and tallow usually used for lame mules made Father's leg better.

9. "I put my trust in the Lord who created them and redeemed them with the most precious Blood of His Son; He will bring them to the fold in the manner and at the time that He will be pleased to do so."

10. Fr. Serra gave thanks that the prayers of St. Joseph saved the whole Mission to Upper California.

11. First, he found a good piece of ground near the sea, and second, he erected and blessed a large Mission cross.

12. Fr. Serra taught the Indians that God loved them, came to earth for them, and died to free them from sin. Our Lord Jesus wanted to bless them with grace in this life and take them to heaven when they died.

13. They learned to grow crops, to raise livestock, to build buildings, to do blacksmithing, to do carpentry, to weave cloth, and to sew clothes.

14. He did so, so that the Indians could take their place as equals in the Spanish society that was sure to come to California.

15. ". . . let us put our confidence in God. He is our Father. He knows what we need and that is enough."

16. "Always go forward, and never turn back."

St. Edith Stein

1. Their main purpose is to gather seven times a day to pray psalms and canticles for the needs of the Church and the conversion of sinners.

2. "Come, Rosa. We are going for our people."

3. Her parents taught their children to honor and help the poor, to dedicate first fruits to God, to do their best in work and study, and to help all in need.

4. Two answers are acceptable: Edith decided to leave school. Edith became an atheist.

5. Phenomenology is the method of arriving at absolute essences through the analysis of living experience.

6. Edith expected to find Anna broken with sorrow, but instead found her full of hope and peace.

7. Edith said, "This is the truth."

8. Edith knew that she needed to be in a Catholic environment for her faith to grow.

9. " ... but the sufferings of Christ. I aspire to share them."

10. The night of November 8-9, 1938 is called Kristallnacht, or "crystal night", for the many broken windows in Jewish synagogues, businesses, and homes.

11. No, they only arrested more Jews. Edith and Rosa were among them.

12. She took care of these children.

Bl. Francis Xavier Seelos

1. Fr. Seelos served at St. Mary's for ten months.

2. He was a holy priest. He was kind in the confessional. He gave sermons in a kind manner. He loved the poor and distressed. He visited sick people, especially the very poor.

3. "I'll be there a year. Then I'll die of yellow fever."

4. Fr. Seelos has served with or been superior to nearly all thirteen Redemptorists in New Orleans. He had come to a house full of old and dear friends.

5. Fr. Seelos was kind, and spoke eloquently of the mercy of God.

6. Fr. Seelos was grateful to his mother for teaching him to practice and to love the Catholic Faith. *or* He was grateful that she taught her children a great devotion to the Mother of God.

7. "So the doctor says I am go die! Oh, what pleasant news! How thankful I am! And to you, doctor, how much I have to return thanks for your kindness and attention to me!"

8. Xavier spent a lot of time with his mother, and she constantly taught him the Catholic Faith. Or His sickness taught him compassion for the sick.

9. He loved to help his father, he served many Masses, and he accompanied his mother to church to say the Rosary. *or* He got to know Fr. Heim, who helped him gain further education.

10. Xavier gave any extra money he had to students who were poorer than he was.

11. He loved his family so much that he feared that seeing them again would make him change his mind.

12. They were impressed with the faithfulness with

which he carried out his priestly duties. *or* He put the faith into practice.

13. He prayed over them before the altar of Our Lady with such confidence that the children were cured of their illness.

14. He did not season his food. He ate whatever was put in front of him. He seemed always to be saying the Rosary in a way that was hardly noticeable. He said the Rosary while traveling. He slept on the floor. When unfairly criticized, he bore it patiently. He said, "Prayer must be my chief strength."

15. First, it was his reliance on prayer, and second, it was his faith in the mercy of God.